Dr. Ackerman's Book of the
Golden Retriever

LOWELL ACKERMAN DVM

BB-103

Overleaf: Every Golden Retriever's favorite place: the lake.

The author has exerted every effort to ensure that medical information mentioned in this book is in accord with current recommendations and practice at the time of publication. However, in view of the ongoing advances in veterinary medicine, the reader is urged to consult with their veterinarian regarding individual health issues.

Photography by Isabelle Francais, Judith P. Iby, Patti Liermann, Jacquelyn Mertens, Scotty Richardson, Penny Shultz, Karen Taylor, and J. Wolff.

The presentation of pet products in this book is strictly for instructive purposes only; it does not necessarily constitute an endorsement by the author, publisher, owners of dogs portrayed, or any other contributors.

© **1996 by LOWELL ACKERMAN DVM**

Distributed in the UNITED STATES to the Pet Trade by T.F.H. Publications, Inc., One T.F.H. Plaza, Neptune City, NJ 07753; distributed in the UNITED STATES to the Bookstore and Library Trade by National Book Network, Inc. 4720 Boston Way, Lanham MD 20706; in CANADA to the Pet Trade by H & L Pet Supplies Inc., 27 Kingston Crescent, Kitchener, Ontario N2B 2T6; Rolf C. Hagen Inc., 3225 Sartelon St. Laurent-Montreal Quebec H4R 1E8; in CANADA to the Book Trade by Vanwell Publishing Ltd., 1 Northrup Crescent, St. Catharines, Ontario L2M 6P5 ; in ENGLAND by T.F.H. Publications, PO Box 15, Waterlooville PO7 6BQ; in AUSTRALIA AND THE SOUTH PACIFIC by T.F.H. (Australia), Pty. Ltd., Box 149, Brookvale 2100 N.S.W., Australia; in NEW ZEALAND by Brooklands Aquarium Ltd. 5 McGiven Drive, New Plymouth, RD1 New Zealand; in Japan by T.F.H. Publications, Japan—Jiro Tsuda, 10-12-3 Ohjidai, Sakura, Chiba 285, Japan; in SOUTH AFRICA by Lopis (Pty) Ltd., P.O. Box 39127, Booysens, 2016, Johannesburg, South Africa. Published by T.F.H. Publications, Inc.

MANUFACTURED IN THE
UNITED STATES OF AMERICA
BY T.F.H. PUBLICATIONS, INC.

CONTENTS

DEDICATION

To my wonderful wife, Susan and my three adorable children, Nadia, Rebecca, and David.

PREFACE

Keeping your Golden Retriever healthy is the most important job that you, as an owner, can do. Whereas there are many books available that deal with breed qualities, conformation, and show characteristics, this may be the only book available dedicated entirely to the preventative health care of the Golden Retriever. This information has been compiled from a variety of sources and assembled here to provide you with the most up-to-date advice available.

This book will take you through the important stages of selecting your pet, screening it for inherited medical and behavioral problems, meeting its nutritional needs, and seeing that it receives optimal medical care.

So, enjoy the book and use the information to keep your Golden Retriever the healthiest it can be for a long, full, and rich life.

Lowell Ackerman DVM

BIOGRAPHY

D
r. Lowell Ackerman is a world-renowned veterinary clinician, author, lecturer, and radio personality. He is a Diplomate of the American College of Veterinary Dermatology and is a consultant in the fields of dermatology, nutrition, and genetics. Dr. Ackerman is the author of 34 books and over 150 book chapters and articles. He also hosts a national radio show on pet health care and moderates a site on the World Wide Web dedicated to pet health care issues (**http://www.familyinternet.com/pet/pet-vet.htm**).

BREED HISTORY

**THE GENESIS OF THE
MODERN GOLDEN RETRIEVER**

The origins of the Golden Retriever are found in Britain in the middle of the 19th century. At that time, a variety of setters and pointers were being bred in the quest for the perfect hunt-ing dog. Early histories of the breed suggested that Sir Dudley Marjoribanks, the first Lord Tweedmouth, bought the first Goldens from a Russian circus

Facing page: Bred to be the perfect hunting dog, the Golden Retriever desires pleasing his master more than anything on earth.

troupe, outcrossed them to diminish their size, and continued to perpetuate the new breed.

This account is colorful but unsubstantiated. The original retrievers likely involved crosses between setters, Newfoundlands and water spaniels. The kennel records of Lord Tweedmouth suggest that he bought a yellow Retriever named Nous in 1865 and bred him to a Tweed Water Spaniel (the breed is now extinct) named Belle. Several more generations of outcrosses (to wavy-coated retrievers, Irish Setters and even a sandy-colored Bloodhound) passed until the "goldens" finally bred true for color.

The first registration of Goldens (then Flat-Coated Retrievers — Golden) by the Kennel Club of England occurred in 1903. The first Golden in Canada was reported in 1881, and by 1890 they were in America as well. The Golden Retriever was finally recognized by the American Kennel Club in 1932 and was considered a "rare breed." From these humble beginnings,

Original retrievers probably involved crosses between setters, Newfoundlands, and water spaniels, but it took a few generations to put the golden color into the Golden Retriever.

A twentieth-century breed, the Golden Retriever ranks among the most beloved of all breeds in the United States and England, where it continues to scale the heights of popularity.

the Golden Retriever has become one of the most popular breeds in the country. The Golden Retriever continues to be extremely popular and has been among the top registered breeds for many years.

MIND &
BODY

**PHYSICAL AND BEHAVIORAL TRAITS
OF THE GOLDEN RETRIEVER**

What defines Golden charac-ter? Golden Re-trievers are reli-able and trustworthy, always ready to listen to problems, instinc-tively knowing when to extend their uncondi-tional friendship. Is it possible to generalize the Golden Re-triever? No, but it is correct to say that a breed member that is

Facing page: The look of love from a healthy, well-cared-for Golden.

not approachable, friendly, and happy to meet you is not a true Golden Retriever. The "Golden" rule is that this breed lives to please and is ever eager to make his owner as happy as he is!

CONFORMATION AND PHYSICAL CHARACTERISTICS

This is not a book about show dogs, so information here will not deal with the conformation of champions and how to select one. The purpose of this chapter is to provide basic information about the stature of the Golden Retriever and qualities of its physical nature.

Clearly, beauty is in the eye of the beholder. Since standards come and standards go, measuring your dog against some imaginary yardstick does little for you or your dog. Just because a dog isn't a show champion doesn't mean that he or she is any less of a family member, and just because a dog is a champion doesn't mean that he or she is not a genetic time bomb waiting to go off.

When breeders and those in-

Never select a puppy for size alone. Golden Retrievers should be medium size dogs, and adults between 60 and 70 pounds fare the best healthwise and huntwise.

Water dogs by definition, Golden Retrievers have a water-resistant coat, rarely need a bath, and need regular brushing to stay mat-free.

terested in showing Golden Retrievers are selecting dogs, they are looking for those qualities that match the breed "standard." This standard, however, is of an imaginary Golden Retriever and it changes from time to time and from country to country. Thus, the conformation and physical characteristics that pet owners should concentrate on are somewhat different and much more practical.

Most adult males are 23–24 inches at the withers, and bitches are about two inches smaller. The normal weight range for the breed is 55–75 pounds (25–35 kg), but a better target is about 60 pounds for females and 65–70 pounds for males. Dogs bred for the show ring tend to be larger and may approach 85–90 pounds. Larger dogs are not necessarily better dogs. Golden Retrievers were never intended to be considered "giants," and the increased size might promote some medical problems that tend to be more common in larger dogs. There is some preliminary evidence that the larger members of the breed might be more susceptible to orthopedic disorders, such as elbow dysplasia and hip dysplasia. Golden Retrievers tend to reach their full adult height by one year of age, but it may be another year or two before they "fill out" and achieve their full adult size.

COAT COLOR, CARE, AND CONDITION

There are several different color variations in the Golden Retriever which reflect preferences of breeders. Those that are breeding for the show ring tend to produce larger dogs that are more blonde, while those working their dogs in the field tend to produce smaller dogs with darker coats. This is just a generalization, of course. Color and coat texture are a matter of esthetics and have nothing to do with health care concerns.

The coat of the Golden Retriever is thick and luxurious and requires regular care. Brushing should be done several times a week or, at the very least, several times a month. Although all dogs shed, Golden Retrievers shed a great deal, and routine brushing is necessary if one has any hope of keeping up with the

The picture of vitality at 14 years of age, AFC Topbrass Gifford of Valhaven retrieves a water fowl and exemplifies the breed's longevity and superior hunting skills. "Giff" owned by Mary Mauer and Kim Martin can pick up 50 birds in a day!

This Golden Retriever puppy, with the blonde coat associated with the show ring, will make somebody a handsome show dog and a loving pet.

situation. If brushing is not done regularly, the coat will mat and require even more work. Mats are especially likely to form in the "feathering" behind the ears, around the tail, and at the hind end.

The best approach is to use a flea comb on the coat every day or every other day. This not only helps to locate fleas but also helps strip away the undercoat before it has time to accumulate. The Golden Retriever is a double-coated breed and should not be bathed excessively. If you are going to bathe your Golden with any regularity, be sure to brush the coat thoroughly first. If not, the matting will be profound and probably require the intervention of a professional groomer.

Golden Retrievers are prone to allergies and to allergic manifestations referred to as "hot spots." The result is a raw weeping area on the skin. The best short-term treatment is to shave the affected area to prevent the problem from advancing. Then, apply soothing water-soluble

An athletic Golden Retriever with his Gumabone® Frisbee®*, the only flying disk made for dogs. It has a bone molded into its chew-worthy polyurethane so that your dog can pick it up easily, even from a smooth surface.

The ideal family member, Golden Retriever Peggy Sue chats with Izzy the cat about home seating arrangements, but Izzy is too stubborn to move off of the comfortable couch.

sprays to offer some temporary pain and itch relief. Ointments and creams are not the best choices for treatment because they can seal the infection in and force it to go deeper. The problem usually resolves within 7—10 days with this form of treatment. Long-term control requires identifying and managing the cause of the allergy.

BEHAVIOR AND PERSONALITY OF THE ACTIVE GOLDEN RETRIEVER

Behavior and personality are two qualities which are hard to standardize within a breed. However, most people would agree that the Golden Retriever is a loving, kind and gentle family pet that lives to please. It enjoys being and working with people.

There are two key concepts in the paragraph above — family

and work. Goldens love being with people; they are family-oriented dogs. They are not happy being "yard dogs" or being isolated from infrequent human contact. They are also working dogs by nature and require a lot of exercise. This makes them unsuitable pets for apartment life or for owners that don't have the time to take them for walks, runs, and other outings. These dogs have a lot of energy and require constructive outlets to burn off steam. Otherwise, they can display neurotic behaviors, such as destructive chewing, eliminating in the house, excessive barking, and stealing family possessions.

The ideal Golden Retriever is neither aggressive nor neurotic but rather a loving family member with good self-esteem and acceptance of position in the family "pack." Because the Golden Retriever is a powerful dog and can cause much damage, it is worth spending the time, when selecting a pup, paying attention to any evidence of personality problems. It is also imperative that *all* Golden Retrievers be obedience trained. Like any other dog, they have the potential to be unruly without appropriate training. Consider obedience class mandatory for your sake and that of your dog. A well-loved and well-controlled Golden Retriever is certain to be a valued family member.

For pet owners, there are several activities to which your Golden Retriever is well-suited. They not only make great walking and jogging partners but are also excellent community volunteers. The breed seems ideally suited to standing still for kisses, hugs and petting that can last for hours at a time. Swimming is a favored pastime, but Goldens don't inherently take to water. Give them an opportunity to advance at their own pace. If you let them swim in your swimming pool, be prepared to clean the filter more often, and make sure your dog knows how to get out of the pool on its own. Never leave a dog unattended in a swimming area—he can drown! The loyal and loving Golden Retriever will be your personal guard dog if properly trained; aggressiveness and viciousness do not fit into the equation.

For Golden Retriever enthusiasts who want to get into more competitive aspects of the dog world, consider these activities: showing, field trialing, obedience, hunting, guarding, tracking, and backpacking.

Last one in the pool...! Swimming is great exercise for your Golden Retriever, but supervision is critical. Teach your dog how to use the ladder so that he can always get out when necessary.

SELECTING

**WHAT YOU NEED TO KNOW TO FIND
THE BEST PUPPY**

Owning the perfect Golden Retriever rarely happens by accident. On the other hand, owning a "genetic dud" is almost always the re-sult of an impulsive purchase and failure to do even basic research. Buying this book is a major step in understanding the situation and making intelligent choices.

Facing page: Golden puppies are easy to acquire; finding a puppy from stock that has been genetically screened will require more time and research.

SOURCES

Recently, a large survey was done to determine whether there were more problems seen in animals adopted from pet stores, breeders, private owners, or animal shelters. Somewhat surprisingly, there didn't appear to be any major difference in total number of problems seen from these sources. What was different were the kinds of problems seen in each source. Thus, you can't rely on any one source because there are no standards by which judgments can be made. Most veterinarians will recommend that you select a "good breeder," but there is no way to identify such an individual. A breeder of champion show dogs may also be a breeder of genetic defects.

The best approach is to select a pup from a source that regularly performs genetic screening and has documentation to prove it. If you are intending to be a pet owner, don't worry about whether your pup is show quality. A mark here or there that might disqualify the pup as a show winner has absolutely no impact on its ability to be a loving and healthy pet. Also, the vast majority of dogs will be neutered and not used for breeding anyway. Concentrate on the things that are important.

MEDICAL SCREENING

Whether you are dealing with a breeder, a breed rescue group, a shelter, or a pet store, your approach should be the same. You want to identify a Golden Retriever that you can live with and screen it for medical and behavioral problems, before you make it a permanent family member. If the source you select has not done the important testing needed, make sure they will offer you a health/temperament guarantee before you remove the dog from the premises to have the work done yourself. If this is not acceptable, or they are offering an exchange-only policy, keep moving; this isn't the right place for you to get a dog. As soon as you purchase a Golden Retriever, pup or adult, go to your veterinarian for a thorough evaluation and testing.

Pedigree analysis is best left to true enthusiasts, but there are some things that you can do even as a novice. Inbreeding is to be discouraged, so check out your four or five generation pedigree and look for names that appear repeatedly. Most breeders line breed, which is acceptable, so you may see the same *prefix* many times but not the same actual dog or bitch. Reputable breeders will usually not allow inbreeding at least three generations back in the puppy's pedigree. Also ask the breeder to provide registration numbers on all ancestors in the pedigree for which testing was done through OFA (Orthopedic Foundation for Animals) and CERF (Canine Eye Registration Foundation). If there are a lot of gaps, the breeder has some explaining to do.

The screening procedure is easier if you select an older dog. Animals can be registered for hips and elbows as young as two years of age by the OFA and by one year of age by Genetic Disease Control (GDC). This is your insurance against hip dysplasia and elbow dysplasia later in life. Golden Retrievers now have a lower incidence of these orthopedic problems than they did previously, because of the efforts of conscientious breeders who have been doing the appropriate testing. A verbal testimonial that they've never heard of the condition in their lines is not adequate and probably means they really don't know if they have a problem — move along.

Evaluation is somewhat more complicated in the Golden Retriever puppy. The PennHip™ procedure can determine the risk for developing hip dysplasia in pups as young as 16 weeks of age. For pups younger than that, you should request copies of OFA or GDC registration for both parents. If the parents haven't both been registered, their hip and elbow status should be considered questionable.

All Golden Retrievers, regardless of age, should be screened for evidence of von Willebrand's disease. This can be accomplished with a simple blood test. The incidence is high enough in the breed that there is no excuse for not performing the test.

For animals older than one year of age, your veterinarian will also want to take a blood sample to check for thyroid function in addition to von Willebrand's disease. Both are common in the Golden Retriever. A heartworm test, urinalysis, and evaluation of feces for internal parasites is also recommended.

Your veterinarian should also perform a very thorough ophthalmologic (eye) examination. The most common eye problems in Golden Retrievers are cataracts, central progressive retinal atrophy, and retinal dysplasia. It is best to acquire a pup whose parents have both been screened for heritable eye diseases and certified "clear" by organizations such as CERF. If this has been the case, an examination by your veterinarian is probably sufficient, and referral to an ophthalmologist is only necessary if recommended by your veterinarian.

BEHAVIORAL SCREENING

Medical screening is important, but don't forget temperament. More dogs are killed each year for behavioral reasons than for all medical problems combined. Temperament testing is a valuable, although not infallible, tool in the screening process. The reason that temperament is so important is that many dogs are eventually destroyed because they exhibit undesirable behaviors. Although not all behaviors are evident in young pups (e.g., aggression often takes many months to manifest itself), detecting anxious and fearful pups (and avoiding them) can be very important in the selection process. Traits most identifiable in the young pup include: fear, excitability, low pain threshold, extreme submission, and noise sensitivity.

Pups can be evaluated for temperament as early as seven to eight weeks of age. Some behaviorists, breeders, and trainers recommend objective testing where scores are given in several different categories. Others are more casual about the process, since it is only a crude indi-

cator anyway. In general, the evaluation takes place in three stages, by someone the pup has not been exposed to. The testing is not done within 72 hours of vaccination or surgery. First, the pup is observed and handled to determine its sociability. Puppies with obvious undesirable traits such as shyness, overactivity, or uncontrollable biting may turn out to be unsuitable. Second, the desired pup is separated from the others and then observed for how it responds when played with and called. Third, the pup should be stimulated in various ways and its responses noted. Suitable activities include lying the pup on its side, grooming it, clipping its nails, gently grasping it around the muzzle, and testing its reactions to noise. In a study conducted at the Psychology Department of Colorado State University, they also found that heart rate was a good indicator in this third stage of evaluation. Actually, they noted the resting heart rate, stimulated the pup with a loud noise, and measured how long it took the heart rate to recover to resting level. Most pups recovered within 36 seconds. Dogs that took considerably longer were more likely to be anxious.

Puppy aptitude tests (PAT)

can be given in which a numerical score is given for 11 different traits, with a 1 representing the most assertive or aggressive expression of a trait and a 6 representing disinterest, independence, or inaction. The traits assessed in the PAT include: social attraction to people, following, restraint, social dominance, el-

ORGANIZATIONS YOU SHOULD KNOW ABOUT

The Orthopedic Foundation for Animals (OFA) is a nonprofit organization established in 1966 to collect and disseminate information concerning orthopedic diseases of animals and to establish control programs to lower the incidence of orthopedic dis-

From aggressive to inactive, pups are evaluated for their temperament. Such tests can help owners become aware of potential behavioral problems; the sooner they are detected, the sooner they can be dealt with.

evation (lifting off ground by evaluator), retrieving, touch sensitivity, sound sensitivity, prey/chase drive, stability, and energy level. Although the tests do not absolutely predict behaviors, they do tend to do well at predicting puppies at behavioral extremes.

eases in animals. A registry is maintained for both hip dysplasia and elbow dysplasia. The ultimate purpose of OFA certification is to provide information to dog owners to assist in the selection of good breeding animals; therefore, attempts to get a dysplastic dog certified will only hurt the breed by perpetuation of the disease. For more information contact your veterinarian or the Orthopedic Foundation for Animals, 2300 Nifong Blvd., Columbia, MO 65201.

The Institute for Genetic Disease Control in Animals (GDC) is a nonprofit organization founded in 1990 and maintains an open registry for orthopedic problems but does not compete with OFA. In an open registry like GDC, owners, breeders, veterinarians, and scientists can trace the genetic history of any particular dog once that dog and close relatives have been registered. At the present time, the GDC operates open registries for hip dysplasia, elbow dysplasia, and osteochondrosis. The GDC are currently developing guidelines for registries of Legg-Calve-Perthes disease, craniomandibular osteopathy, and medial patellar luxation. For more information, contact the Institute for Genetic Disease Control in Animals, P.O. Box 222, Davis, CA 95617.

The Canine Eye Registration Foundation (CERF) is an international organization devoted to eliminating hereditary eye

X-rays are the only way to guarantee the presence of hip dysplasia. The Golden Retriever is necessarily anesthetized to undergo this procedure. Not until the dog is two years old can definitive results be secured.

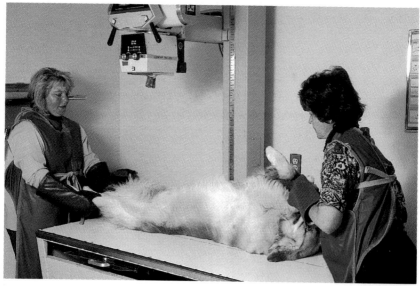

diseases from purebred dogs. This organization is similar to OFA that helps eliminate disease like hip dysplasia. CERF is a nonprofit organization that screens and certifies purebreds as free of heritable eye diseases. Dogs are evaluated by veterinary eye specialists, and findings are then submitted to CERF for documentation. The goal is to identify purebreds without heritable eye problems so they can be used for breeding. Dogs being considered for breeding programs should be screened and certified by CERF on an annual basis, since not all problems are evident in puppies. For more information on CERF, write to CERF, SCC-A, Purdue University, West Lafayette, IN 47907.

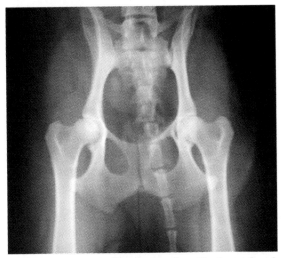

This radiograph displays a dog that received an OFA "excellent" when x-rayed for hip dysplasia. Both of his hip joints are clear of dysplasia.

Project TEACH™ (Training and Education in Animal Care and Health) is a voluntary accreditation process for those individuals selling animals to the public. It is administered by Pet Health Initiative, Inc. (PHI) and provides instruction on genetic screening as well as many other aspects of proper pet care. TEACH-accredited sources screen animals for a variety of medical, behavioral, and infectious diseases *before* they are sold. Project TEACH™ supports the efforts of registries such as OFA, GDC, and CERF and recommends that all animals sold be registered with the appropriate agencies. For more information on Project TEACH™, send a self-addressed stamped envelope to Pet Health Initiative, P.O. Box 12093, Scottsdale, AZ 85267-2093.

FEEDING AND NUTRITION

**WHAT YOU MUST CONSIDER EVERY DAY TO FEED
YOUR GOLDEN RETRIEVER THROUGH HIS LIFETIME**

Nutrition is one of the most important aspects of raising a healthy Golden Retriever, and yet it is often the source of much controversy between breeders, veterinarians,

pet owners, and dog food manufacturers. However, most of these arguments have more to do with marketing than with science. Let's first take

Facing page:
Golden
Retrievers need a
sound diet to
maintain good
health.

28

a look at dog foods and then determine the needs of our dog. This chapter will concentrate on feeding the pet Golden Retriever rather than breeding or working Goldens.

COMMERCIAL DOG FOODS

Most dog foods are sold based on marketing (i.e., how to make a product appealing to owners while meeting the needs of dogs). Some foods are marketed on the basis of their protein content, others based on a "special" ingredient, and still others are sold because they don't contain certain ingredients (e.g., preservatives, soy). We want a dog food that specifically meets our dog's needs, is economical, and causes few, if any, problems. Most foods come in dry, semi-moist, and canned forms. Some can now be purchased frozen. The "dry" foods are the most economical containing the least fat and the most preservatives. The canned foods are the most expensive (they're 75% water) usually containing the most fat and least preservatives. Semi-moist foods are expensive and high in sugar content, and I do not recommend them for any dogs.

When you're selecting a commercial diet, make sure the food has been assessed by feeding trials for a specific life stage, not just by nutrient analysis. This statement is usually located near the ingredient label. In the United States, these trials are performed in accordance with American Association of Feed Control Officials (AAFCO), and in Canada, by the Canadian Veterinary Medical Association. This certification is important because it has been found that dog foods currently on the market, that provide only a chemical analysis and calculated values but no feeding trial, may not provide adequate nutrition. The feeding trials show that the diets meet minimal, not optimal standards; however, they are the best tests we currently have.

PUPPY REQUIREMENTS

Soon after pups are born, and certainly within the first 24 hours, they should begin nursing their mother. This provides them with colostrum, an antibody-rich milk that helps protect them from infection for their first few months of life. Pups should be allowed to nurse for at least six weeks before they are completely weaned from their mother. Supplemental feeding may be started by as early as three weeks of age.

By two months of age, pups should be fed puppy food. They are now in an important growth phase. Nutritional deficiencies and/or imbalances during this time of life are more devastating than at any other time. Also, this is not the time to overfeed pups or provide them with "performance" rations. Overfeeding Golden Retrievers can lead to serious skeletal defects such as osteochondrosis and hip dysplasia.

Pups should be fed "growth" diets until they are 12–18 months of age. Many Golden Retrievers do not mature until 18–24 months of age and so benefit from a longer period on these rations. Pups will initially need to be fed two to three meals daily until they are 12–18 months old, then once to twice daily (preferably twice) when they are converted to adult food. Proper growth diets should be selected based on acceptable feeding trials designed for growing pups. If you can't tell by reading the label, ask your veterinarian for feeding advice.

Remember that pups need "balance" in their diets. Avoid the temptation to supplement with protein, vitamins, or minerals. Calcium supplements have been implicated as a cause of bone and cartilage deformity, especially in large breed puppies. Puppy diets are already heavily fortified with calcium,

and supplements tend to unbalance the mineral intake. There is more than adequate proof that these supplements are responsible for many bone deformities seen in these growing dogs.

ADULT DIETS

The goal of feeding adult dogs is one of "maintenance." They have already done all the grow-

Going in the trash can mean that your Golden is bored or hungry. Consider whether or not you are feeding him a balanced diet: he may instinctively be looking for a little extra calcium! Some Golden are always hungry, so never overindulge a chow hound.

ing they are going to do and are unlikely to have the digestive problems of elderly dogs. In general, dogs can do well on maintenance rations containing predominantly plant or animal-based ingredients, as long as that ration has been specifically formulated to meet maintenance level requirements. This contention should be supported by studies performed by the manufacturer in accordance with AAFCO. In Canada, these products should be certified by the Canadian Veterinary Medical Association to meet maintenance requirements.

There's nothing wrong with feeding a cereal-based diet to dogs on maintenance rations; they are the most economical. When comparing maintenance rations, it must be appreciated that these diets must meet the "minimal" requirements for confined dogs, not necessarily optimal levels. Most dogs will benefit when fed diets that contain easily-digested ingredients that provide nutrients at least slightly above minimal requirements. Typically, these foods will be intermediate in price between the most expensive super-premium diets and the cheapest generic diets. Select only those diets that have been substantiated by feeding trials to meet maintenance requirements, those that contain wholesome ingredients, and those recommended by your veterinarian. Don't select based on price alone, on company advertising, or on total protein content.

GERIATRIC DIETS

Golden Retrievers are considered elderly when they are about seven years of age. There are certain changes that occur as dogs age that alter their nutritional requirements. As pets age, their metabolism slows and must be accounted for. If maintenance rations are fed in the same amounts while metabolism is slowing, weight gain may result. Obesity is the last thing one wants to contend with in an elderly pet, since it increases their risk of several other health-related problems. As pets age, most of their organs do not function as well as in youth. The digestive system, liver, pancreas, and gallbladder are not functioning at peak effect. The intestines have more difficulty extracting all the nutrients from the food consumed. A gradual decline in kidney function is considered a normal part of aging.

A responsible approach to geriatric nutrition is to realize that degenerative changes are a normal part of aging. Our goal is to minimize the potential damage done by taking this into account while the dog is still well. If we wait until an elderly dog is ill before we change the diet, we have a much harder job.

Elderly dogs need to be treated as individuals. While some benefit from the nutrition found in "senior" diets, others might do better on the highly-digestible puppy or super-premium diets. These latter diets provide an excellent blend of digestibility and amino acid content, but unfortunately, many are higher in salt and phosphorus than the older pet really needs.

Older dogs are also more prone to developing arthritis, and therefore, it is important not to overfeed them, since obesity puts added stress on the joints. For animals with joint pain, supplementing the diet with fatty acid combinations containing cis-linoleic acid, gamma-linolenic acid, and eicosapentaenoic acid can be quite beneficial.

MEDICAL CONDITIONS AND DIET

It is important to keep in mind that dietary choices can affect the development of orthopedic diseases such as hip dysplasia and osteochondrosis. When feeding a pup at risk, avoid high-calorie diets and try to feed several times a day rather than ad libitum. Sudden growth spurts are to be avoided because they result in joint instability. Recent research has also suggested that the electrolyte balance of the diet may also play a role in the development of hip dysplasia. Rations that had more balance between the positively and nega-

Roar-Hide™ dog chews made by Nylabone® are a safe alternative to traditional rawhide. They also help reduce plaque and tartar build-up.

tively charged elements in the diet (e.g., sodium, potassium, chloride) were less likely to promote hip dysplasia in susceptible dogs. Also, avoid supplements of calcium, phosphorus, and vitamin D as they can interfere with normal bone and cartilage development. The fact is that calcium levels in the body are carefully regulated by hormones (such as calcitonin and parathormone) as well as vitamin D. Supplementation disturbs this normal regulation and can cause many problems. It has also been shown that calcium supplementation can interfere with the proper absorption of zinc from the intestines. If you really feel the need to supplement your dog, select products such as eicosapentaenoic/gamma-linolenic fatty acid combinations or small amounts of vitamin C.

Diet can't prevent bloat (gastric dilatation-volvulus), but changing feeding habits can make a difference. Initially, the bloat occurs when the stomach becomes distended with swallowed air. This air is swallowed as a consequence of gulping food or water, stress, and exercising too close to mealtime. This is where we can make a difference. Divide meals and feed them three times daily rather than all at once. Soak dry dog

By putting dog food on an elevated surface, you help reduce your Golden Retriever's risk of gastric dilation/volvulus or bloat. Bloat is life threatening, so take the necessary precautions.

food in water before feeding to decrease the tendency to gulp the food. If you want to feed dry food only, add some large clean chew toys to the feed bowl so that the dog has to "pick" to get at the food and can't gulp it. Putting the food bowl on a step-stool, so the dog doesn't have to stretch to get the food, may also be helpful. Finally, don't allow any exercise for at least one hour before and after feeding.

Thornfield's General Sherman, like all dogs, needs a constant supply of fresh water. As with food, keeping water elevated prevents your dog from gulping thus reducing the risk of bloat.

Fat supplements are probably the most common supplements purchased from pet supply stores. They frequently promise to add luster, gloss, and sheen to the coat and consequently make dogs look healthy. The only fatty acid that is essential for this purpose is cis-linoleic acid, which is found in flaxseed oil, sunflower seed oil, and safflower oil. Corn oil is a suitable, but less effective, alternative. Most of the other oils found in retail supplements are high in saturated and monounsaturated fats and are not beneficial for shiny fur or healthy skin. For dogs with aller-gies, arthritis, high blood pressure (hypertension), high cholesterol, and some heart ailments, other fatty acids may be prescribed by a veterinarian. The important ingredients in these products are gamma-linolenic acid (GLA), eicosapentaenoic acid (EPA), and docosahexaenoic acid (DHA). These products have gentle and natural anti-inflammatory properties. But don't be fooled by imitations. Most retail fatty acid supplements do not contain these functional forms of the essential fatty acids—look for gamma-linolenic acid, eicosapentaenoic acid, and docosahexaenoic acid on the label.

HEALTH

**PREVENTIVE MEDICINE AND HEALTH
CARE FOR YOUR GOLDEN RETRIEVER**

Keeping your Golden Retriever healthy requires preventive health care. This is not only the most effective but the least expensive way to battle illness.

Good preventive care starts even before puppies are born. The dam should be well cared for, vaccinated, and free of infections and parasites. Hopefully, both

Facing page: You owe it your Golden, for the unconditional love and friendship he affords you, to provide the health care possible.

36

parents were screened for important genetic diseases (e.g., von Willebrands's disease), were registered with the appropriate agencies (e.g., OFA, GDC, CERF), showed no evidence of medical or behavioral problems, and were found to be good candidates for breeding. This gives the pup a good start in life. If all has been planned well, the dam will pass on resistance to disease to her pups that will last for the first few months of life. However, the dam can also pass on parasites, infections, genetic diseases, and more.

TWO TO THREE WEEKS OF AGE

By two to three weeks of life, it is usually necessary to start pups on a regimen to control worms. Although dogs benefit from this parasite control, the primary reason for doing this is human health. After whelping, the dam often sheds large numbers of worms even if she tested negative previously. This is because many worms lay dormant in tissues and the stress of delivery causes parasite release into the environment. Assume that all puppies potentially have worms because studies have shown that 75% do. Thus, we institute worm control early to protect the people in the house from worms more than the pups themselves.

The deworming is repeated every two to three weeks until your veterinarian feels the condition is under control. Nursing bitches should be treated at the same time because they often shed worms during this time. Only use products recommended by your veterinarian. Over-the-counter parasiticides have been responsible for deaths in pups.

SIX TO TWENTY WEEKS OF AGE

Most puppies are weaned from their mother at six to eight weeks of age. Weaning shouldn't be done too early, so that pups have the opportunity to socialize with their littermates and dam. This is important for them to be able to respond to other dogs later in life. There is no reason to rush the weaning process, unless the dam can't produce enough milk to feed the pups.

Pups are usually first examined by their veterinarian at six to eight weeks of age, which is when most vaccination schedules commence. If pups are exposed to many other dogs at this young age, veterinarians often opt for vaccinating with inactivated parvovirus at six weeks of age. When exposure isn't a factor, most veterinarians would rather wait to see the pup at eight weeks of age. At this point, they can also do a preliminary dental evaluation to see that all the puppy teeth are coming in correctly, check to see that the testicles are properly descending in males and that there are no health reasons to prohibit testing on the pup by eight weeks of age, or recommend someone to do it for you. Although temperament testing is not completely accurate, it can often predict which pups are most anxious and fearful. Some form of

Regularity is probably the most important aspect of good preventive health care. Sharlow's Irish Sundancer CD, Delta Dog is not only checked regularly, but helps check children with owner Neva Sharlow, RN, OCN.

vaccination at this time. Heart murmurs, wandering knee-caps (luxating patellae), juvenile cataracts, persistent pupillary membranes (a congenital eye disease), and hernias are usually evident by this time.

Your veterinarian may also be able to perform temperament temperament evaluation is important because behavioral problems account for more animals being euthanized (killed) each year than all medical conditions combined.

Recently, some veterinary hospitals have been recommending neutering pups as early as six to eight weeks of age. A study done at the University of Florida, College of Veterinary Medicine over a span of more than four years concluded there was no increase in complications when animals were neutered when less than six months of age. The evaluators also concluded that the surgery appeared to be less stressful when done in young pups.

Most vaccination schedules consist of injections being given at 6–8, 10–12, and 14–16 weeks of age. Ideally, vaccines should not be given closer than two weeks apart, and three to four weeks seems to be optimal. Each vaccine usually consists of several different viruses (e.g., parvovirus, distemper, parainfluenza, hepatitis) combined into one injection. Coronavirus can be given as a separate vaccination according to this same schedule, if pups are at risk. Some veterinarians and breeders advise another parvovirus booster at 18–20 weeks of age. A booster is given for all vaccines at one year of age and annually thereafter. For animals at increased risk of exposure, parvovirus vaccination may be given as often as four times a year. A new vaccine for canine cough (tracheobronchitis) is squirted into the nostrils. It can be given as early

as six weeks of age, if pups are at risk. Leptospirosis vaccination is given in some geographic areas and likely offers protection for six to eight months. The initial series consists of three to four injections spaced two to three weeks apart, starting as early as ten weeks of age. Rabies vaccine is given as a separate injection at three months of age, then repeated when the pup is one year old, then every one to three years depending upon local risk and government regulation.

Between 8 and 14 weeks of age, use every opportunity to expose the pup to as many people and situations as possible. This is part of the critical socialization period that will determine how good a pet your dog will become. This is not the time to abandon a puppy for eight hours while you go to work. This is also not the time to punish your dog in any way, shape, or form.

This is the time to introduce your dog to neighborhood cats, birds, and other creatures. Hold off on exposure to other dogs until after the second vaccination in the series. You don't want your new friend to pick up contagious diseases from dogs it meets in its travels. By 12 weeks of age, your pup should be ready for social outings with other dogs. Do it! It's a great way for your dog to feel comfortable around members of its own species. Walk the streets and introduce your pup to everybody you meet. Your goal should be to introduce your dog to every type of person or situation it is likely to encounter in its life. Take it in cars, elevators, buses, subways, parade grounds, and beaches. You want it to habituate to all environments. Expose your pup to kids, teenagers, old people, people in wheelchairs, people on bicycles, people in uniforms, etc. The more varied the exposure, the better the socialization.

The best way to be sure that your dog is safe from becoming lost is identification tags. Microchip implantation and tattooing are other options.

Proper identification of your pet is also important, since this minimizes the risk of theft and increases the chances that your pet will be returned to you if it is lost. There are several different options. Microchip implantation is a relatively painless procedure involving the subcutaneous injection of an implant the size of a grain of rice. This implant does not act as a beacon if your pet is missing. However, if your pet turns up at a veterinary clinic or shelter and is checked with a scanner, the chip provides information about you that can be used to quickly reunite you with your pet. This method of identification is reasonably priced, permanent in nature, and performed at most veterinary clinics. Another option is tattooing which can be done on the inner ear or on the skin of the abdomen. Most purebreds are given a number by the associated registry (e.g., American Kennel Club, The Kennel Club, United Kennel Club, Canadian Kennel Club, etc.) that is used for identification. Alternatively, permanent numbers, such as social security numbers (telephone numbers and addresses may change during the life of your pet), can be used in the tattooing process. There are several different tattoo registries maintaining lists of dogs, their tattoo codes, and their owners. Finally, identifying collars and tags provide quick information but can be separated from your pet if it is lost of stolen. They work best when combined with a permanent identification system such as microchip implantation or tattooing.

FOUR TO SIX MONTHS OF AGE

At 16 weeks of age, when your pup gets the last in its series of regular induction vaccinations, ask your veterinarian about evaluating the pup for hip dysplasia with the PennHip™ technique. This helps predict the risk of developing hip dysplasia as well as degenerative joint disease. Golden Retriever breeders have done an excellent job decreasing the incidence of hip dysplasia through routine screening and registration programs, but they still have a long way to go. Since anesthesia is typically required for the procedure, many veterinarians like to do the evaluation at the same time as neutering.

At this time, it is very worthwhile to perform a diagnostic test for von Willebrand's disease, an inherited disorder that causes uncontrolled bleeding. This trait is fairly common in the Golden

Retriever. A simple blood test is all that is required, but it may need to be sent to a special laboratory to have the test performed. You will be extremely happy you had the foresight to have this done before neutering. If your dog does have a bleeding problem, it will be necessary to take special precautions during surgery. This is also a great time to run the parvovirus antibody titer to determine how well your dog has responded to the vaccination series.

SIX TO TWELVE MONTHS OF AGE

As a general rule, neuter your animal at about six months of age unless you fully intend to breed it. As we know, neutering can be safely done at eight weeks of age, but this is still not a common practice. Neutering not only stops the possibility of pregnancy and undesirable behaviors but can prevent several health problems as well. It is a well-established fact that pups spayed before their first heat have a dramatically reduced incidence of mammary (breast) cancer. Likewise, neutered males significantly decrease their incidence of prostate disorders.

When your pet is six months of age, your veterinarian will want to take a blood sample to perform a heartworm test. If the test is negative and shows no evidence of heartworm infection, the pup will go on heartworm prevention therapy. Some veterinarians are even recommending preventive therapy in younger pups. This might be a once-a-day regimen, but newer therapies can be given on a once-a-month basis. As a bonus, most of these heartworm preventatives also help prevent internal parasites.

Another part of the six-month visit should be a thorough dental evaluation to make sure all the permanent teeth have correctly erupted. If they haven't, this will be the time to correct the problem. Correction should only be performed to make the animal more comfortable and promote normal chewing. The procedures should never be used to cosmetically improve the appearance of a dog used for show purposes or breeding.

After the dental evaluation, you should start implementing home dental care. In most cases, this will consist of brushing the teeth one or more times each week and perhaps using dental rinses. It is a sad fact that 85% of dogs over four years of age have periodontal disease and "doggy breath." In fact, it is so common that most people think it is "nor-

mal." Well, it is normal — as normal as bad breath would be in people if they never brushed their teeth. Brush your dog's teeth regularly with a special toothbrush and toothpaste, and you can greatly reduce the incidence of tartar buildup, bad breath, and gum disease. Provide the Puppybone® from Nylabone® and a Gumabone® to puppies as early as eight to ten weeks. Nylabones® not only help in the proper development of the puppy's jaw and the emergence of adult teeth but help to keep the teeth clean...and the breath fresh. Better preventive care means that dogs live a long time, and they'll enjoy their sunset years more if they still have their teeth. Ask your veterinarian for details on home dental care.

THE FIRST SEVEN YEARS

At one year of age, your dog should be re-examined again and have boosters for all vaccines. Your veterinarian will also want to do a very thorough physical examination to look for early evidence of problems. This might include taking radiographs (x-rays) of the hips and elbows to look for evidence of dysplastic changes. Genetic Disease Control (GDC) will certify hips and elbows at 12 months of

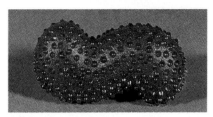

Golden Retrievers, which have strong jaws, do well with Hercules™ by Nylabone®, designed for dogs with powerful chewing ability.

age; Orthopedic Foundation for Animals won't issue certification until 24 months of age.

At 12 months of age, it's also a great time to have some blood samples analyzed to provide background information. Although few Golden Retrievers experience clinical hypothyroidism at this young age, the process may be starting. Therefore, it is a good idea to have baseline levels of thyroid hormones (free and total), thyroid-stimulating hormone (TSH), autoantibodies, blood cell counts, organ chemistries, and cholesterol levels. This can serve as a valuable comparison to samples collected in the future.

Each year after that, preferably around the time of your pet's birthday, it's time for another veterinary visit. This visit is a wonderful opportunity for a thorough clinical examination, rather than just "shots." Since

85% of dogs have periodontal disease by four years of age, veterinary intervention does not seem to be as widespread as it should be. The examination should include visually inspecting the ears, eyes (a great time to start scrutinizing for progressive retinal atrophy, cataracts, etc.), mouth (don't wait for gum disease), and groin; listening (auscultation) to the lungs and heart; feeling (palpating) the lymph nodes and abdomen; and answering all of your questions about optimal health care. In addition, booster vaccinations are given during these times, feces are checked for parasites, urine is analyzed, and blood samples may be collected for analysis. One of the tests run on the blood sample is for heartworm antigen. In areas of the country where heartworm is only present in the spring, summer, and fall (it's spread by mosquitoes), blood samples are collected and evaluated about a month prior to the mosquito season. Other routine blood tests are for blood cells (hematology), organ chemistries, thyroid levels, and electrolytes.

By two years of age, most veterinarians prefer to begin preventive dental cleanings, often referred to as "prophies." Anesthesia is required, and the veterinarian or veterinary dentist will use an ultrasonic scaler to remove plaque and tartar from above and below the gum line, as well as polish the teeth so that plaque has a harder time sticking to the teeth. Radiographs (x-rays) and fluoride treatments are other options. It is now known that it is plaque, not tartar, that initiates inflammation in the gums. Since scaling and root planing remove more tartar than plaque, veterinary dentists have begun using a new technique called PerioBUD (periodontal bactericidal ultrasonic debridement). The ultrasonic treatment is quicker, disrupts more bacteria, and is less irritating to the gums. With tooth polishing to finish up the procedure, gum healing is better, and owners can start home care sooner. Each dog has its own dental needs that must be addressed, but most veterinary dentists recommend prophies annually. Be sure too that your

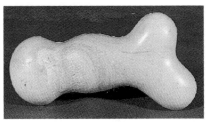

Nylabone's® Galileo™ is the toughest nylon pacifier available. Its unique shape succeeds in keeping the dog from breaking or chipping the bone.

Golden Retriever always has a Nylabone® available to do his part in keeping his teeth clean.

SENIOR GOLDEN RETRIEVERS

Golden Retrievers are considered seniors when they reach about seven years of age. Usually, veterinarians still only need to examine them once a year, but it is now important to start screening for geriatric problems. Accordingly, blood profiles, urinalysis, chest radiographs (x-rays), and electrocardiograms (EKG) are recommended on an annual basis. When problems are caught early, they are much more likely to be successfully managed. This is as true in canine medicine as it is in human medicine.

Raised dental tips on dog bones work wonders with controlling plaque in a Golden Retriever. Only get the largest Plaque Attacker™ for your Golden.

MEDICAL PROBLEMS

**RECOGNIZED GENETIC CONDITIONS
SPECIFICALLY RELATED TO THE GOLDEN RETRIEVER**

M any conditions appear to be especially prominent in Golden Retrievers. Sometimes it is possible to identify the genetic basis of a problem, but in many cases, we must be satisfied with merely identifying the breeds that are a risk and how the

Facing page: Visit your veterinarian as often as he indicates. Vets can administer tests to make sure your dog is clear of possibly life-threatening hereditary and congenital conditions. This is especially crucial if you're considering breeding.

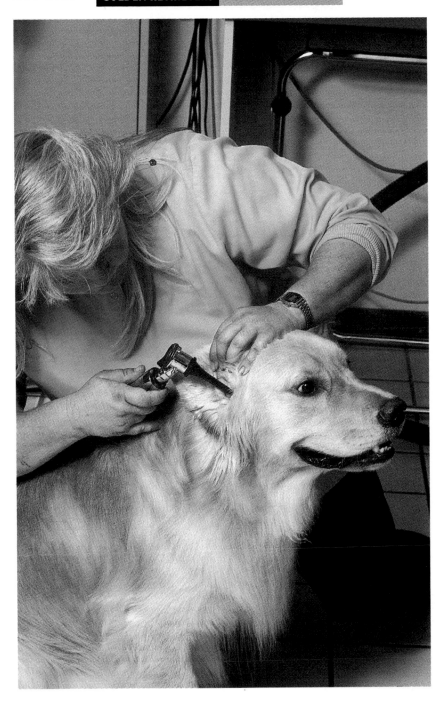

conditions can be identified, treated, and prevented. Following are some conditions that have been recognized as being common in the Golden Retriever, but this listing is certainly not complete. Also, many genetic conditions may be common in certain breed lines, not in the breed in general.

AORTIC STENOSIS

Aortic stenosis is a hereditary heart disease characterized by an obstruction below the aortic valve. At least two genes are involved in the process, one of which is dominant. Because of the pattern of inheritance, there tends to be a family history of the problem. Many pups may appear fine at first, while others may exhibit weakness, fainting, or even sudden death. The diagnosis can be made relatively easily by thorough veterinary examination with a stethoscope (auscultation), x-rays (radiography), electrocardiography (ECG), and/or ultrasound examination (echocardiography). Some mildly affected animals may be fine without therapy, while others require medications (e.g., beta blockers) or corrective surgery by six months of age. Thorough examination of the parents will determine (in most cases) the responsible in-

dividual. Even normal littermates should not be used in breeding programs.

CATARACTS

Cataracts refer to an opacity or cloudiness on the lens of the eye, and ophthalmologists are careful to categorize them on the basis of stage, age of onset, and location. In Golden Retrievers, the pattern of inheritance of cataracts has not been determined. However, they are prone to two different types that can be seen in juveniles or adults. Perinuclear cataracts tend to be progressive, while the posterior subcapsular cataracts tend to be non-progressive. Since these cataracts are not usually evident in puppies, they are typically missed on initial examinations. Many dogs adapt well to cataracts, but cataract removal surgery is available and quite successful if needed. The condition may be associated with persistent hyperplastic primary vitreous. Affected animals and their siblings should obviously not be used for breeding, and careful ophthalmologic evaluation of both parents is warranted.

CILIARY DYSKINESIA

Primary ciliary dyskinesia, also known as immotile cilia syndrome and Kartagener's syndrome, refers to a condition in which the hair-like cilia in the respiratory passages cannot perform their needed defense mechanisms. Primary ciliary dyskinesia is believed to be inherited in people as an autosomal recessive trait, but the genetics have not been confirmed in the dog.

The most common clinical manifestation of ciliary dyskinesia is recurring chronic respiratory infection. Therefore, affected dogs often cough, may develop a runny nose, have poor exercise tolerance, and sometimes have fever. The result is often bronchitis and pneumonia. The tails (flagellae) of sperm are modified cilia, so it is not surprising that many dogs with primary ciliary dyskinesia are infertile. Approximately half of affected dogs has internal organs that are transposed to the wrong side of the body. Some affected individuals also have hearing loss, middle ear infections, and dysfunction of some of their white blood cells (neutrophils) needed to fight off infection.

The best way to confirm a diagnosis of primary ciliary dyskinesia is with special biopsies submitted for electron microscope evaluation or mucociliary clearance with a radiation counter. Both are involved procedures. In most cases, the diagnosis is suspected when a young animal gets recurrent respiratory infections that respond to antibiotics but recur soon after the drug is discontinued. With mature intact males, sperm can be evaluated for defective sperm motility. This is not an absolute test because some dogs may have

The eyes of the Golden Retriever should be clear and bright like this dog's. An opacity or cloudiness on the lens may indicate the presence of a potential problem.

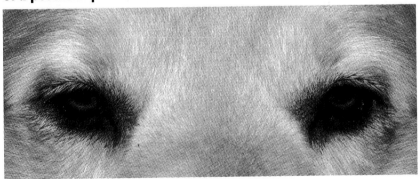

normal-appearing sperm yet still have the condition. In about 50% of cases, chest radiographs will reveal the heart on the right side of the chest.

There is no cure for primary ciliary dyskinesia. Symptomatic therapy includes periodic antibiotics based on culture results. Cough suppressants should not be used, since they further impede normal defense mechanisms. If the infections can be maintained under reasonable control, affected dogs stand a chance of living a relatively normal existence. Affected dogs, their littermates, and their parents should not be used in breeding programs.

ELBOW DYSPLASIA

Elbow dysplasia doesn't refer to just one disease, but rather an entire complex of disorders that affect the elbow joint. Several different processes might be involved, including ununited anconeal process, fragmented medial coronoid process, osteochondritis of the medial humeral condyle, or incomplete ossification of the humeral condyle. Elbow dysplasia and osteochondrosis are disorders of young dogs, with problems usually starting between four and seven months of age. The usual manifestation is a sudden onset of lameness. In time, the continued inflammation results in arthritis in those affected joints.

Golden Retrievers are often listed as being particularly prone to elbow dysplasia. Statistics compiled by the Orthopedic Foundation for Animals found that 10.8% of males and 8.8% of females of the Golden Retriever breed, assessed up until December 31, 1994, have evidence of elbow dysplasia on radiographs (x-rays). Continued registration is recommended to further lessen the incidence by conscientious breeding.

Radiographs (x-rays) are taken of the elbow joints and submitted to a registry for evaluation. The Orthopedic Foundation for Animals (OFA) will assign a breed registry number to those animals with normal elbows that are over 24 months of age. Abnormal elbows are reported as grade I to III, where grade III elbows have well-developed degenerative joint disease (arthritis).

Facing page: Every Golden Retriever deserves a fair shake. Choose a puppy from stock that has been screened for genetic problems. Responsible breeding establishments never breed without screening.

Normal elbows on individuals 24 months or older are assigned a breed registry number and are periodically reported to parent breed clubs. Genetic Disease Control for Animals (GDC) maintains an open registry for elbow dysplasia and assigns a registry number to those individuals with normal elbows at 12 months of age or older. Only animals with "normal" elbows should be used for breeding.

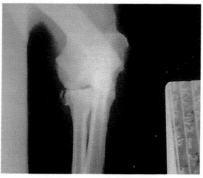

Fragmented coronoid process of the elbow, a manifestation of elbow dysplasia. Courtesy of Dr. Jack Henry.

There is strong evidence to support the contention that OCD of the elbow is an inherited disease likely controlled by many genes. Preliminary research (in Labrador Retrievers) also suggests that the different forms of elbow dysplasia are inherited independently. Therefore, breeding stock should be selected from those animals without a history of osteochondrosis, preferably for several generations. Unaffected dogs producing offspring with OCD, FCP (fragmented coronoid process), or both should not be bred again, and unaffected first-degree relatives (e.g., siblings) should not be used for breeding either.

Other than genetics, the most likely associations made to date suggest that feeding diets high in calories, calcium, and protein promote the development of osteochondrosis in susceptible dogs. Also, animals that are allowed to exercise in an unregulated fashion are at increased risk, since they are more likely to sustain cartilage injuries.

The management of dogs with OCD is a matter of much debate and controversy. Some recommend surgery to remove the damaged cartilage before permanent damage is done. Others recommend conservative therapy of rest and pain-killers. The most common drugs used are aspirin and polysulfated glycosaminoglycans. Most veterinarians agree that the use of cortisone-like compounds (corticosteroids) creates more problems than it treats in this condition. What seems clear is that some dogs will respond to conservative therapies, while other need surgery. Surgery is often helpful if performed before there is significant joint damage.

EPILEPSY

Idiopathic epilepsy runs in families, and breeding studies have shown a genetic basis for the disorder. It is most often first seen in dogs between one and three years of age. The condition is similar to that reported in people, and the seizures follow the same pattern.

The generalized seizure usually involves certain phases. The aura is the first phase. In this phase the animal may appear restless, fearful, abnormally affectionate, or show other behavioral changes. The ictus phase, the actual seizure phase, follows the aura. Here the animal usually loses consciousness, and its limbs become stiff. This is followed by paddling movements of the limbs. Crying, urination, defecation, and salivation may also occur. This phase may last from seconds to minutes. The final phase is post-ictus. During this phase one may see confusion, circling, blindness, or sleepiness. It may last from several minutes to a few days. There is no apparent correlation between the length of the post-ictus phase and the length or severity of the ictus phase.

The diagnosis is made by pairing a history of seizures with normal test results for other potential causes. The most common anti-seizure medication used in veterinary medicine is phenobarbital, which is very good at preventing seizures and has few side effects. The animal may have an increase in appetite and thirst and, occasionally, temporary weakness while becoming accustomed to the drug. It is important to periodically check the level of phenobarbitol in the blood. This is done by taking a blood sample immediately before giving the anticonvulsant medication so the concentration of drug is measured when lowest. This blood level shows whether the amount of drug given needs to be increased, decreased, or remain the same. Primidone and potassium bromide are considered options for animals that don't respond well to phenobarbital. Although complete elimination of seizure activity may not be achieved, it is still important to reduce the seizures in both intensity and frequency as much as possible. Affected animals should not be used for breeding.

GASTRIC DILATATION/ VOLVULUS

Gastric dilatation (bloat) occurs when the stomach becomes distended with air. The air gets swallowed into the stomach when susceptible dogs exercise, gulp their food/water, or are stressed. Although bloat can occur at any age, it becomes more common as susceptible dogs get older. Purebreds are three times more likely to suffer from bloat than mutts. Although Golden Retrievers are susceptible to the condition and frequently appear in lists of "breeds most prone to bloat," recent large surveys haven't found that Golden Retrievers are as prone as other deep-chested breeds such as Great Danes, Weimaraners, Saint Bernards, Gordon Setters, Irish Setters, Boxers, and Standard Poodles.

Bloat on its own is uncomfortable, but it is the possible consequences that make it life-threatening. As the stomach fills with air, like a balloon, it can twist on itself and impede the flow of food within the stomach as well as the blood supply to the stomach and other digestive organs. This twisting (volvulus or torsion) not only makes the bloat worse but also results in toxins being released into the bloodstream and death of blood-deprived tissues. These events, if allowed to progress, will usually result in death in four to six hours. Approximately one-third of dogs with bloat and volvulus

Know your dog's habits—sleeping, eating, and playing. If the dog is acting abnormal, listless, and irritable, there could be a problem.

will die, even under appropriate hospital care.

Affected dogs will be uncomfortable, restless, depressed, and have an extended abdomen. They need veterinary attention immediately, or they will suffer from shock and die! There are a variety of surgical procedures to correct the abnormal positioning of the stomach and organs. Intensive medical therapy is also necessary to treat for shock, acidosis, and the effects of toxins.

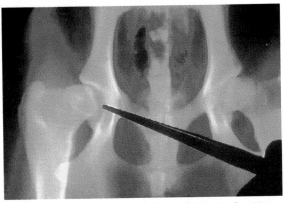

Radiograph of a dog with hip dysplasia. Note the flattened femoral head at the marker. Courtesy of Toronto Academy of Veterinary Medicine, Toronto, Canada.

Bloat can't be completely prevented, but there are some easy things to do to greatly reduce the risk. Don't leave food down for dogs to eat as they wish. Divide the day's meals into three portions and feed morning, afternoon, and evening. Try not to let your dog gulp its food; if necessary, add some chew toys to the bowl so he has to work around them to get the food. Add water to dry food before feeding. Have fresh clean water available all day but not at mealtime. Do not allow exercise for one hour before and after meals. Following this feeding advice may actually save your dog's life. In addition to this information, there has been no studies that support the contention that soy in the diet increases the risk of bloat. Soy is relatively poorly digested and can lead to flatulence, but the gas accumulation in bloat comes from swallowed air, not gas produced in the intestines.

HIP DYSPLASIA

Hip dysplasia is a genetically transmitted developmental problem of the hip joint that is common in many breeds. Dogs may be born with a "susceptibility" or "tendency" to develop hip dysplasia, but it is not a foregone conclusion that all susceptible dogs will eventually develop hip dysplasia. All dysplastic dogs are born with normal hips, and the dysplastic changes begin within the first 24 months of life, although they are usually evident long before then.

It is now known that there are several factors that help determine whether a susceptible dog will ever develop hip dysplasia. These include body size, conformation, growth patterns, caloric load, and electrolyte balance in the dog food.

Golden Retrievers are often cited as being prone to hip dysplasia. Based on research tabulated up to January, 1995, the Orthopedic Foundation for Animals concluded that 22.6% of the radiographs submitted from Golden Retrievers had evidence of hip dysplasia. This is a high incidence, but Golden Retriever breeders have been able to reduce the incidence in the breed by over 20–30% just through conscientious breeding.

When purchasing a Golden Retriever pup, it is best to ensure that the parents were both registered with normal hips through one of the international registries such as the Orthopedic Foundation for Animals or Genetic Disease Control. Pups over 16 weeks of age can be tested by veterinarians trained in the PennHip™ procedure, which is a way of predicting risk of devel-

oping hip dysplasia and arthritis. In time it should be possible to completely eradicate hip dysplasia from the breed.

If you start with a pup with less risk of hip dysplasia, you can further reduce your risk by controlling its environment. Select a food with a moderate amount of protein, and avoid the super high premium and high-calorie diets. Also, feed your pup several times a day for defined periods (e.g., 15 minutes) rather than leaving the food down all day. Avoid all nutritional supplements, especially those that include calcium, phosphorus, and/or vitamin D. Use controlled exercise for your pup rather than letting him run loose. Unrestricted exercise in the pup can stress the joints which are still developing.

If you have a dog with hip dysplasia, all is not lost. There is much variability in the clinical presentation. Some dogs with severe dysplasia experience little pain, while others that have minor changes may be extremely sore. The main problem is that dysplastic hips promote degenerative joint disease (osteoarthritis or osteoarthrosis), which can eventually incapacitate the joint. Aspirin and other anti-inflammatory agents are suitable in the early stages. Surgery is needed when animals are in great pain, when drug therapy doesn't work adequately, or when movement is severely compromised.

HYPOTHYROIDISM

Hypothyroidism is the most commonly diagnosed endocrine (hormonal) problem in the Golden Retriever. The disease itself refers to an insufficient amount of thyroid hormones being produced. Although there are several different potential causes, lymphocytic thyroiditis is by far the most common. Iodine deficiency and goiter are extremely rare. In lymphocytic thyroiditis, the body produces antibodies that target aspects of thyroid tissue. The process usually starts between one and three years of age in affected animals but doesn't become clinically evident until later in life.

There is a great deal of misinformation about hypothyroidism. Owners often expect their dog to be obese and otherwise don't suspect the condition. The fact is that hypothyroidism is quite variable in its manifestations, and obesity is only seen in a small percentage of cases. In most cases, affected animals appear fine until they use up most of their remaining thyroid hormone reserves. The most common manifestations then are lack of energy and recurrent infections. Hair loss is seen in about one-third of cases.

You might suspect that hypothyroidism would be easy to diagnose, but it is trickier than you think. Since there is a large reserve of thyroid hormones in the body, a test measuring only total blood levels of the hormones (T-4 and T-3) is not a very sensitive indicator of the condition. Thyroid stimulation tests are the best way to measure the functional reserve. Measuring "free" and "total" levels of the hormones is another approach. Also, since we know that most cases are due to antibodies produced in the body, screening for these autoantibodies can help identify animals at risk of developing hypothyroidism. A new endogenous TSH (thyroid-stimulating hormone) test is also now available and is very helpful in identifying dogs with problems early.

Because this breed is so prone to developing hypothyroidism, periodic screening for the disorder is warranted in many cases. Although none of the screening tests is perfect, a basic panel evaluating total T-4, free T-4, TSH, and cholesterol levels is a good start. Ideally, this would first be performed at one year of age and annually thereafter. This screening is practical because none of these tests is very expensive.

Fortunately, although there may be some problems in diagnosing hypothyroidism, treatment is straightforward and relatively inexpensive. Supplementing the affected animal twice daily with thyroid hormones effectively treats the condition. Animals with hypothyroidism should not be used in a breeding program, and those with circulating autoantibodies, but no actual hypothyroid disease, should also not be used for breeding.

INHALANT ALLERGIES

Inhalant allergy (atopy) is the canine version of hay fever and is extremely common. The Golden Retriever is likely the breed most commonly affected with allergies, and they are extremely prevalent in this breed. Whereas people with allergies often sneeze, dogs with allergies scratch—they're itchy. The most common manifestations include licking and chewing at the front feet. There may also be face rubbing, a rash on the belly or in the armpits, and subsequent bacterial infections on the skin surface. The offenders are molds, pollens, and house dust that are

Outdoor events can expose your puppy to fleas, grass molds, and pollen that may cause an allergy....even in this first-place Golden!

present in the air. Most dogs start to have problems some time after six months of age. Hot spots are focal areas of infection that result secondary to allergic reactions. In most cases, the cause is inhalant allergies, but food allergies, flea bite hypersensitivity, ear problems, and anal sac disorders can all cause hot spots as well.

Allergies are diagnosed in dogs similar to the way they are diagnosed in people. Intradermal (skin) testing is the most specific test and is usually done by veterinary dermatologists or others in referral settings. Blood tests are also available for allergy testing but are, at present, less reliable.

Mild cases of allergy can be treated with antihistamines, fatty acid supplements (combinations of eicosapentaenoic acid and gamma-linolenic acid), and frequent soothing baths. Allergies that last for more than three to four months each year, or are severe, are best treated with immunotherapy (allergy shots). Corticosteroids effectively reduce the itch of allergy but can cause other medical problems with long-term use.

The only effective way of preventing inhalant allergies is to select pups from parents that aren't allergic themselves. This is a complicated process, since animals may be bred before they are old enough to show evidence of allergies.

PROGRESSIVE RETINAL ATROPHY

Progressive retinal atrophy (PRA) refers to several inherited disorders affecting the retina that result in blindness. PRA is thought to be inherited, with each breed demonstrating a specific age of onset and pattern of inheritance. Golden Retrievers tend to have an age of onset of about two years. Therefore, when pups are first evaluated, they typically show no evidence of the problem. A related condition, central progressive retinal atrophy, is also commonly reported in the Golden Retriever, especially those in Great Britain.

All of the conditions described as progressive retinal atrophy have one thing in common — there is progressive atrophy or degeneration of the retinal tissue. Visual impairment occurs slowly, but progressively. Therefore, animals often adapt to their reduced vision until it is compromised to near blindness. Because of this, owners may not notice any visual impairment until the condition has progressed significantly.

Progressive retinal atrophy encompasses both degenerative and dysplastic varieties. Retinal dysplasia refers to malformation in the retinal tissue during fetal development and is the most common form of PRA in the Golden Retriever.

The diagnosis of PRA can be made in two ways: direct visualization of the retina and electroretinography (ERG). The use of indirect ophthalmoscopy requires a great deal of training and expertise and is more commonly performed by ophthalmology specialists than general practitioners. The other highly sensitive test, usually available only from specialists, is electroretinography. This instrument measures electrical patterns in the retina the same way an ECG measures electrical activity of the heart. The procedure is painless, but usually available only from specialty centers. This instrument is sensitive enough to detect even the early onset of disease.

Unfortunately there is no treatment available for progressive retinal atrophy. Since most dogs are presented very late in the course of the disease, they are often blind at the time of diagnosis. Identification of affected breeding animals is essential to prevent spread of the condition within the breed. Dogs from breeds at increased risk should be examined annually by a veterinary ophthalmologist. Because Golden Retrievers tend not to be affected as pups, it is necessary for them to be re-evaluated when they are mature (two years of age).

SEBACEOUS ADENITIS

Sebaceous adenitis is a recently described inflammatory disease of the hair follicles and the sebaceous glands that supply them. Most animals are in young adulthood when first affected and develop flaking of the skin and then a loss of hair. In general, the condition is not itchy or irritating, unless the dogs have managed to develop infection in these sites. Other than these changes, the dogs appear to remain in good health.

For proper diagnosis, biopsies are required, and they should be sent to veterinary pathologists with expertise in skin disorders. Therapy of early cases is often attempted with corticosteroids, but success is variable. Other treatments being evaluated include: vitamin A derivatives (retinoids), antibiotics, cyclosporine, and essential fatty-acid supplements. Topical treatment is important because the skin becomes very dry and scaly. This means frequent shampooing with products that help remove surface scale (e.g., tar, salicylic acid, selenium sulfide) and improving the moisture content of the skin with rinses of 50% propylene glycol and various other moisturizers, emollients, and humectants. There is no cure, and affected animals should definitely not be used for breeding.

VON WILLEBRAND'S DISEASE

The most commonly inherited bleeding disorder of dogs is von

Willebrand's disease (vWD). The abnormal gene can be inherited from one or both parents. If both parents pass on the gene, most of the resultant pups fail to thrive and will die. In most cases, however, the pup inherits a relative lack of clotting ability, which is quite variable. For instance, one dog may have 15% of the clotting factor, while another might have 60%. The higher the amount, the less likely it will be that the bleeding will be readily evident, since spontaneous bleeding is usually only seen when dogs have less than 30% of the normal level of von Willebrand clotting factor. Thus, some dogs don't get diagnosed until they are neutered or spayed, and they end up bleeding uncontrollably or they develop pockets of blood (hematomas) at the surgical site.

Because the incidence appears to be on the rise, von Willebrand's disease is extremely important in the Golden Retriever, however, there is good news. There are tests available to determine the amount of von Willebrand factor in the blood that are accurate and reason-

Bennington Hills Zachary CDX, CGC stands with dignity on the beach. The only happy Golden is a healthy active one.

ably priced. Goldens used for breeding should have normal amounts of von Willebrand factor in their blood, and so should all pups that are adopted as household pets. Carriers should not be used for breeding, even if they appear clinically normal. Since hypothyroidism can be linked with von Willebrand's disease, thyroid profiles can also be a useful part of the screening procedure in older Goldens.

SOME OTHER CONDITIONS MORE COMMONLY SEEN IN THE GOLDEN RETRIEVER

- Acral lick dermatitis
- Cerebellar abiotrophy
- Coloboma of optic nerve
- Corneal dystrophy
- Diabetes mellitus
- Distichiasis
- Ectropion
- Enophthalmos
- Entropion
- Ichthyosis
- Iris cysts
- Juvenile cellulitis
- Muscular dystrophy
- Optic nerve hypoplasia
- Osteosarcoma
- Peripheral hypomyelination
- Persistent pupillary membranes
- Portosystemic shunt
- Seborrhea
- Uveodermatologic syndrome

The Golden Retriever's body must be in excellent shape to endure the robust activity for which the breed is known. In great shape are Starburst Show Em Some Magic CD, CGC and Bennington Hills Zachary CDX, CGC as they spend the afternoon retrieving and playing in a local lake.

INFECTIONS & INFESTATIONS

**HOW TO PROTECT YOUR
GOLDEN RETRIEVER FROM PARASITES AND MICROBES**

An important part of keeping your Golden Retriever healthy is to prevent problems caused by parasites and microbes. Although there are drugs available that can help limit problems, prevention is always the desired option, leading to less aggravation, less itch, and expense.

Facing page: Combing regularly helps keep the coat looking its best and controls the flea population.

Fleas are a common nuisance to dogs. The best way to keep fleas off of your dog is to exterminate them from your immediate surroundings.

FLEAS

Fleas are important and common parasites but not an inevitable part of every pet-owner's reality. If you take the time to understand some of the basics of flea population dynamics, control is both conceivable and practical.

Fleas have four life stages (egg, larva, pupa, adult), and each stage responds to some therapies while being resistant to others. Failing to understand this is the major reason why some people have so much trouble getting the upper hand in the battle to control fleas.

Fleas spend all their time on the host animal (in this case, your dog) and only leave if physically removed by brushing, bathing, or scratching. However, the eggs that are laid on the animal are not sticky and fall to the ground to contaminate the environment. Our goal must be to remove fleas from the animals in the house, from the house itself, and from the immediate outdoor environment. Part of our plan must also involve using different medications to get rid of the different life stages, as well as minimizing the use of potentially harmful insecticides that could be poisonous for pets and family members.

A flea comb is a very handy device for recovering fleas from pets. The best places to comb are the tailhead, groin area, armpits, back, and neck region. Fleas collected should be dropped into a container of alcohol which quickly kills them before they can escape. In addition, all pets should be bathed with a cleansing shampoo (or flea shampoo) to remove fleas and eggs. This, however, has no residual effect, and fleas can jump back on immediately after the bath if nothing else is done. Rather than using potent insecticidal dips and sprays, consider products containing the safe pyrethrins (derived from chrysanthemums) and the insect growth regulators (such as methoprene and fenoxycarb). These products are not only extremely safe, but the combination is effective against eggs, larvae and adults. This only leaves the pupal stage to cause continued problems. Insect growth regulators can also be safely given as once-a-month oral preparations. Flea collars are rarely useful, and electronic flea collars are not to be recommended for any dogs.

Vacuuming is a good first step to cleaning up the household because it picks up about 50% of the flea eggs and it also stimulates flea pupae to emerge as adults, a stage when they are easier to kill with insecticides. The vacuum bag should then be removed and discarded with each treatment. Household treatment can then be initiated with pyrethrins and a combination of either insect growth regulators or sodium polyborate (a borax derivative). The pyrethrins need to be reapplied every two to three weeks, but the insect growth regulators last about two to three months, and many companies guarantee sodium polyborate for a full year. Stronger insecticides, such as carbamates and organophosphates, can be used and will last three to four weeks in the household, but they are potentially toxic and offer no real advantages other than their persis-

tence in the home environment (this is also one of their major disadvantages).

When an insecticide is combined with an insect growth regulator, flea control is most likely to be successful. The insecticide kills the adult fleas, and the insect growth regulator affects the eggs and larvae. However, insecticides kill less than 20% of flea cocoons (pupae). Because of this, new fleas may hatch in two to three weeks despite appropriate application of prod-

Flea control isn't an easy task, and even after this puppy is washed and dried, fleas can jump right back on. Remember to treat the whole environment.

ucts. This is known as the "pupal window," and is one of the most common causes for ineffective flea control. This is why a safe insecticide should be applied to the home environment two to three weeks after the initial treatment. This catches the newly hatched pupae before they have a chance to lay eggs and perpetuate the flea problem.

If treatment of the outdoor environment is needed, there are several options. Fenoxycarb, an insect growth regulator, is stable in sunlight and can be used outdoors. Sodium polyborate can be used as well, but it is important that it not be inadvertently eaten by pets. Organophosphates and carbamates are sometimes recommended for outdoor use, and it is not necessary to treat the entire property. Flea control should be directed predominantly at garden margins, porches, dog houses, garages, and in other pet lounging areas. Fleas don't do well with direct exposure to sunlight so generalized lawn treatment is not needed. Finally, microscopic worms (nematodes) are available that can be sprayed onto the lawn with a garden sprayer. The nematodes eat immature flea forms and then biodegrade without harming anything else.

TICKS

Ticks are found world wide and can cause a variety of problems including blood loss, tick paralysis, Lyme disease, "tick fever," Rocky Mountain spotted fever, and babesiosis. All are important diseases which need to be prevented whenever possible. This is only possible by limiting the exposure of our pets to ticks.

For those species of tick that dwell indoors, the eggs are laid mostly in cracks and on vertical surfaces in kennels and homes. Otherwise most other species are found outside in vegetation, such as grassy meadows, woods, brush, and weeds.

Ticks feed only on blood, but they don't actually bite. They attach to an animal by sticking their harpoon-shaped mouth parts into the animal's skin, and then they suck blood. Some ticks can increase their size 20—50 times as they feed. Favorite places for them to locate are between the toes and in the ears, although they can appear anywhere on the skin surface.

A good approach to prevent ticks is to remove underbrush and leaf litter, and to thin the trees in areas where dogs are allowed. This removes the cover and food sources for small mammals that serve as hosts for ticks.

Ticks must have adequate cover that provides high levels of moisture and at the same time provides an opportunity of contact with animals. Keeping the lawn well maintained also makes ticks less likely to drop by and stay. Because of the potential for ticks to transmit a variety of harmful diseases, dogs should be carefully inspected after walks through wooded areas (where ticks may be found), and careful removal of all ticks is very important in the prevention of disease. Care should be taken not to squeeze, crush, or puncture the body of the tick, since exposure to body fluids of ticks may lead to spread of any disease carried by that tick to the animal or to the person removing the tick. The tick should be disposed of in a container of alcohol or flushed down the toilet. If the site becomes infected, veterinary attention should be sought immediately. Insecticides and repellents should only be applied to pets following appropriate veterinary advice, since indiscriminate use can be dangerous. Recently, a new tick collar has become available which contains amitraz. This collar not only kills ticks but causes them to retract from the skin within two to three days. This greatly reduces the chances of ticks

Ixodes scapularis, **the deer tick, is the most dangerous to your dog and yourself because it transmits Lyme disease. Courtesy of Virbac Labora-tories, Inc., Fort Worth, Texas.**

transmitting a variety of diseases. A spray formulation has also recently been developed and marketed. It might seem that there should be vaccines for all the diseases carried by ticks, but only a Lyme disease *(Borrelia burgdorferi)* formulation is currently available.

MANGE

Mange refers to any skin condition caused by mites. The contagious mites include ear mites, scabies mites, cheyletiella mites, and chiggers. Demodectic mange is associated with proliferation of demodex mites, but they are not considered contagious.

The most common causes of mange in dogs are ear mites, which are extremely contagious. The best way to avoid ear mites is to buy pups from sources that don't have a problem with ear mite infestation. Otherwise, pups readily acquire them when kept in crowded environments in which other animals might be carriers. Treatment is effective if whole body (or systemic) therapy is used, but relapses are common when medication in the ear canal is the only approach. This is because the mites tend to crawl out of the ear canal when medications are instilled. They simply feed elsewhere on the body until it is safe for them to return to the ears.

Scabies mites and cheyletiella mites are passed on by other dogs that are carrying the mites. They are "social" diseases that can be prevented by avoiding exposure of your dog to others that are infested. Scabies (sarcoptic mange) has the dubious honor of being the most itchy disease to which dogs are susceptible. Chigger mites are present in forested areas, and dogs acquire them by roaming in these areas. All can be effectively diagnosed and treated by your veterinarian should your dog happen to become infested.

HEARTWORM

Heartworm disease is caused by the worm *Dirofilaria immitis* and is spread by mosquitoes. The female heartworms produce microfilariae (baby worms) that circulate in the bloodstream, waiting to be picked up by mosquitoes to pass the infection along. Dogs do not get heartworm by socializing with infected dogs; they only get infected by mosquitoes that carry the infective microfilariae. The adult heartworms grow in the heart and major blood vessels and eventually cause heart failure.

Fortunately, heartworm is easily prevented by safe oral medications that can be administered daily or on a once-a-month basis. The once-a-month preparations also help prevent many of the common intestinal parasites, such as hookworms, roundworms, and whipworms.

Prior to giving any preventative medication for heartworm, an antigen test (an immunologic test that detects heartworms) should be performed by a veterinarian, since it is dangerous to give the medication to dogs that harbor the parasite. Some experts also recommend a microfilarial test just to be doubly certain. Once the test results show that the dog is free of heartworms, the preventative therapy can be commenced. The length of time the heartworm preventatives must be given depends on the length of the mosquito season. In some parts of the country, dogs are on preventative therapy year round. Heartworm vaccines may soon be available, but the preventatives now available are easy to administer, inexpensive, and quite safe.

INTESTINAL PARASITES

The most important internal parasites in dogs are roundworms, hookworms, tapeworms, and whipworms. Roundworms are the most common. It has been estimated that 13 trillion roundworm eggs are discharged in dog feces every day! Studies have shown that 75% of all pups carry roundworms and start shedding them by three weeks of age. People are infected by exposure to dog feces containing infective roundworm eggs, not by handling pups. Hookworms can cause a disorder known as cutaneous larva migrans in people. In dogs, they are most dangerous to puppies, since they latch onto the intestines and suck blood. They can cause anemia and even death when they are present in large numbers. The most common tapeworm is *Dipylidium caninum* which is spread by fleas. However, another tapeworm *(Echinococcus multilocularis)* can cause fatal disease in people and can be spread to people from dogs. Whipworms live in the lower

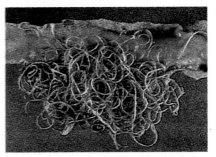

The most common intestinal parasite, roundworms are found in 75% of all pups. People can also be infected with roundworms by simply cleaning up after their dog's feces.

aspects of the intestines. Dogs get whipworms by consuming infective larvae. However, it may be another three months before they start shedding them in their stool, greatly complicating diagnosis. In other words, dogs can be infected by whipworms, but fecal evaluations are usually negative until the dog starts passing those eggs three months after being infected.

Other parasites, such as coccidia, cryptosporidium, giardia, and flukes can also cause problems in dogs. The best way to prevent all internal parasite problems is to have pups dewormed according to your veterinarian's recommendations and parasite checks done on a regular basis, at least annually.

VIRAL INFECTIONS

Dogs get viral infections such as distemper, hepatitis, parvovirus, and rabies by exposure to infected animals. The key to prevention is controlled exposure to other animals and, of course, vaccination. Today's vaccines are extremely effective, and properly vaccinated dogs are at minimal risk for contracting these diseases. However, it is still important to limit exposure to other animals that might be harboring infection. When selecting a facility for boarding or grooming an animal, make sure they limit their clientele to animals that have documented vaccine histories. This is in everyone's best interest. Similarly, make sure your veterinarian has a quarantine area for infected dogs and that animals aren't admitted for surgery, boarding, grooming, or diagnostic testing without up-to-date vaccinations. By controlling exposure and ensuring vaccination, your pet should be safe from these potentially devastating diseases.

It is beyond the scope of this book to settle all the controver-

Why are these dogs smiling? Well it is probably because Magic, Mario, Zachary, and Sherman know they are safer fenced in rather than free to run into danger.

These rescue Golden Retrievers are doing a charity walk to help other Golden Retrievers. We can help by choosing our dog with care and committing to caring for him for his whole life.

sies of vaccination, but they are worth mentioning. Should vaccines be combined in a single injection? It's convenient and cheaper to do it this way, but might some vaccine ingredients interfere with others? Some say yes, some say no. Are vaccine schedules designed for convenience or effectiveness? Mostly convenience. Some ingredients may only need to be given every two or more years, research is incomplete. Should the dose of the vaccine vary with weight, or should a Chihuahua receive the same dose as a Golden Retriever? Good questions, no definitive answers. Finally, should we be using modified-live or inactivated vaccine products? There is no short answer for this debate. Ask your veterinarian, and do a lot of reading yourself!

CANINE COUGH

Canine infectious tracheobronchitis, also known as canine cough and kennel cough, is a contagious viral/bacterial disease that results in a hacking cough that may persist for many weeks. It is common wherever dogs are kept in close quarters, such as kennels, pet stores, grooming parlors, dog shows, training classes, and even veterinary clinics. The condition doesn't respond well to most medications, but eventually clears spontaneously over the course of many weeks. Pneumonia is a possible but uncommon complication.

Prevention is best achieved by limiting exposure and utilizing vaccination. The fewer opportunities you give your dog to come in contact with others, the less the likelihood of getting infected. Vaccination is not foolproof because many different viruses can be involved. Parainfluenza virus is included in most vaccines and is one of the more common viruses known to initiate the condition. *Bordetella bronchiseptica* is the bacterium most often associated with tracheobronchitis, and a vaccine is available that needs to be repeated twice yearly for dogs at risk. This vaccine is squirted into the nostrils to help stop the infection before it gets deeper into the respiratory tract. Make sure the vaccination is given several days (preferably two weeks) before exposure for maximum protection.

Dogs that participate in field trials—like these amazing Topbrass Goldens—must be vaccinated for canine cough, commonly spread where there are many dogs congregated.

This Golden Retriever with his Gumabone® Frisbee®* couldn't be happier. Provide your dog with safe play things that are designed for dogs and won't become easily frayed or broken.

FIRST AID
by Judy Iby, RVT

**KNOWING YOUR DOG IN GOOD HEALTH
& BEING PREPARED FOR EMERGENCIES**

With some experience, you will learn how to give your dog a physical at home and consequently, will learn to recognize many potential problems. If you can  detect a problem early, you can seek timely medical help and thereby decrease your dog's risk of developing a more serious problem.

Facing page: You must know your puppy's moods and behavior so that you can decide when to take him to the veterinarian. Avi Zechory, DVM can show Magic's owner how to check the dog's vital signs.

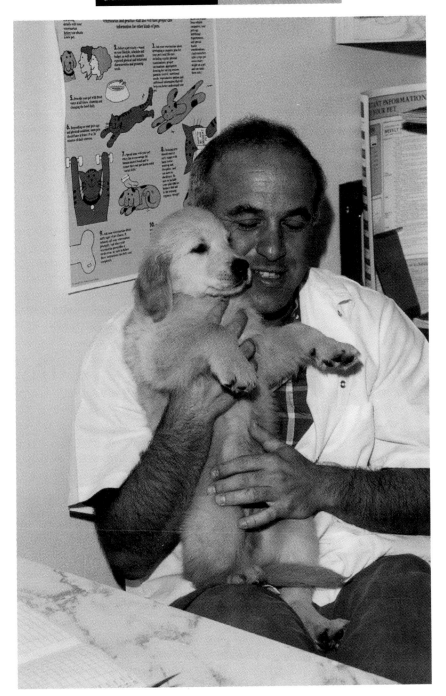

Every pet owner should be able to take his pet's temperature, pulse, respirations and check the capillary refill time (CRT). Knowing what is normal will alert the pet owner to what is abnormal, and this can be life saving for the sick pet.

TEMPERATURE

The dog's normal temperature is 100.5 – 102.5 degrees Fahrenheit. Take the temperature rectally for at least one minute. Be sure to shake the thermometer down first, and you may find it helpful to lubricate the end. It is easy to take the temperature with the dog in a standing position. Be sure to hold on to the thermometer so that it isn't expelled or sucked in. A dog could have an elevated temperature if he is excited or if he is overheated; however, a high temperature could indicate a medical emergency. On the other hand, if the temperature is below 100 degrees, this could also indicate an emergency.

Learn some of the techniques that can save your dog's life in case of an emergency. From taking the dog's pulse to performing CPR, you can make a difference in your dog's life.

If your Golden Retriever won't eat, it could be an indication that he is sick. Unless the weather is very hot or the dog is sexually distracted, loss of appetite may indicate cause for alarm.

CAPILLARY REFILL TIME AND GUM COLOR

It is important to know how your dog's gums look when he is healthy, so you will be able to recognize a difference if he is not feeling well. There are a few breeds, among them the Chow Chow and its relatives, that have black gums and a black tongue. This is normal for them. In general, a healthy dog will have bright pink gums. Pale gums are an indication of shock or anemia and are an emergency. Likewise, any yellowish tint is an indication of a sick dog. To check capillary refill time (CRT), press your thumb against the dog's gum. The gum will blanch out (turn white) but should refill (return to the normal pink color) in one to two seconds. CRT is very important. If the refill time is slow and your dog is acting poorly, you should call your veterinarian immediately.

HEART RATE, PULSE, AND RESPIRATIONS

Heart rate depends on the breed of the dog and his health. Normal heart rates range from about 50 beats per minute in the larger breeds to 130 beats per minute in the smaller breeds. You can take the heart rate by pressing your fingertips on the dog's chest. Count for either 10 or 15 seconds, and then multiply by either 6 or 4 to obtain the rate per minute. A normal pulse is the same as the heart rate and is taken at the femoral artery located on the insides of both rear legs. Respirations should be observed and depending on the size and breed of the dog, should be 10 – 30 per minute. Obviously, illness or excitement could account for abnormal rates.

PREPARING FOR AN EMERGENCY

It is a good idea to prepare for an emergency by making a list and keeping it by the phone. This list should include:
1. Your veterinarian's name, address, phone number, and office hours.
2. Your veterinarian's policy for after-hour care. Does he take his own emergencies or does he refer them to an emergency clinic?
3. The name, address, phone number and hours of the emergency clinic your veterinarian uses.
4. The number of the National Poison Control Center for Animals in Illinois: 1-800-548-2423. It is open 24 hours a day.

In a true emergency, time is of the essence. Some signs of an emergency may be:
1. Pale gums or an abnormal heart rate.
2. Abnormal temperature, lower than 100 degrees or over 104 degrees.
3. Shock or lethargy.
4. Spinal paralysis.

A dog hit by car needs to be checked out and probably should have radiographs of the chest and abdomen to rule out pneumothorax or ruptured bladder.

EMERGENCY MUZZLE

An injured, frightened dog may not even recognize his owner and may be inclined to bite. If your dog should be injured, you may need to muzzle him to protect yourself before you try to handle him. It is a good idea to practice muzzling the calm, healthy dog so you understand the technique. Slip a lead over his head for control. You can tie his mouth shut with

An injured dog can be traumatized and not recognize his owner. An emergency muzzle is safest for the dog and you.

something like a two-foot-long bandage or piece of cloth. A necktie, stocking, leash or even a piece of rope will also work.

1. Make a large loop by tying a loose knot in the middle of the bandage or cloth.
2. Hold the ends up, one in each hand.
3. Slip the loop over the dog's muzzle and lower jaw, just behind his nose.
4. Quickly tighten the loop so he can't open his mouth.
5. Tie the ends under his lower jaw.
6. Make a knot there and pull the ends back on each side of his face, under the ears, to the back of his head.

If he should start to vomit, you will need to remove the muzzle immediately. Otherwise, he could aspirate vomitus into his lungs.

ANTIFREEZE POISONING

Antifreeze in the driveway is a potential killer. Because antifreeze is sweet, dogs will lap it up. The active ingredient in antifreeze is ethylene glycol, which causes irreversible kidney damage. If you witness your pet ingesting antifreeze, you should call your veterinarian immediately. He may recommend that you induce vomiting at once by using hydrogen peroxide, or he may recommend a test to confirm antifreeze ingestion. Treatment is aggressive and must be administered promptly if the dog is to live, but you wouldn't want to subject your dog to unnecessary treatment.

BEE STINGS

A severe reaction to a bee sting (anaphylaxis) can result in difficulty breathing, collapse and even death. A symptom of a bee sting is swelling around the muzzle and face. Bee stings are antihistamine responsive. Over-the-counter antihistamines are available and many may be administered at 1mg per pound every six hours for three treatments. You should monitor the dog's gum color and respirations and watch for a decrease in swelling. If your dog is showing signs of anaphylaxis, your veterinarian may need to give him an injection of corticosteroids. It would be wise to call your veterinarian and confirm treatment.

BLEEDING

Bleeding can occur in many forms, such as a ripped dewclaw, a toenail cut too short, a puncture wound, a severe laceration, etc. If a pressure bandage is needed, it must be released every 15–20 minutes. Be careful of elastic bandages since it is easy to apply them too tightly. Any bandage material should be clean. If no regular bandage is available, a small towel or wash cloth can be used to cover the wound and bind it with a necktie, scarf, or something similar. Styptic powder, or even a soft cake of soap, can be used to stop a bleeding toenail. A ripped dewclaw or toenail may need to be cut back by the veterinarian and possibly treated with antibiotics. Depending on their severity, lacerations and puncture wounds may also need professional treatment. Your first thought should be to clean the wound with peroxide, soap and water, or some other antiseptic cleanser. Don't use alcohol since it deters the healing of the tissue.

Facing page: The "good ole' summertime" seems just a memory. Goldens, like most other dogs, don't prefer to be outdoors in the summer heat. Heatstroke is a very real threat to dogs, and shade is tantamount to survival. Never leave the dog outdoors without ample shade and plenty of water.

BLOAT

Although not generally considered a first aid situation, bloat can occur in a dog rather suddenly. Truly, it is an emergency! Gastric dilation-volvulus or gastric torsion—the twisting of the stomach to cut off both entry and exit, causing the organ to "bloat" —is a disorder primarily found in the larger, more deep-chested breeds. It is life threatening and requires immediate veterinary assistance.

BURNS

If your dog gets a chemical burn, call your veterinarian immediately. Rinse any other burns with cold water and if the burn is significant, call your veterinarian. It may be necessary to clip the hair around the burn so it will be easier to keep clean. You can cleanse the wound on a daily basis with saline and apply a topical antimicrobial ointment, such as silver sulfadiazine 1 percent cream or gentamicin cream. Burns can be debilitating, especially to an older pet. They can cause pain and shock. It takes about three weeks for the skin to slough after the burn and there is the possibility of permanent hair loss.

CARDIOPULMONARY RESUSCITATION (CPR)

Check to see if your dog has a heart beat, pulse and spontaneous respiration. If his pupils are already dilated and fixed, the prognosis is less favorable. This is an emergency situation which requires two people to adminis-

On any dog hit by a car, it is a good idea to routinely x-ray the chest and abdomen.

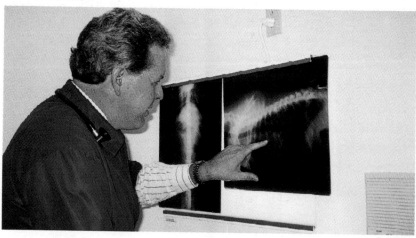

The knowledge of first aid is essential if you are going to take you Golden Retriever into the woods. Be prepared and carry a kit if you are going on a long hike.

ter lifesaving techniques. One person needs to breathe for the dog while the other person tries to establish heart rhythm. Mouth–to–mouth resuscitation starts with two initial breaths, 1–1.5 seconds in duration. After the initial breaths, breathe for the dog once after every five chest compressions. (You do not want to expand the dog's lungs while his chest is being compressed.) You inhale, cover the dog's nose with your mouth, and exhale *gently*. You should see the dog's chest expand. Sometimes, pulling the tongue forward stimulates respiration. You should be ventilating the dog 12–20 times per minute. The person managing the chest compressions should have the dog lying on his right side with one hand on either side of the dog's chest, directed over the heart between the fourth and fifth ribs (usually this is the point of the flexed elbow). The number of compressions administered depends on the size of the patient. Attempt 80–120 compressions per minute. Check for spontaneous respiration and/or heart beat. If present, monitor the patient and discontinue resuscitation. If you haven't already done so, call your veterinarian at once and make arrangements to take your pet in for professional treatment.

CHOCOLATE TOXICOSIS

Dogs like chocolate, but chocolate kills dogs. Its two basic chemicals, caffeine and theobromine, overstimulate the dog's nervous system. Ten ounces of milk chocolate can kill a 12–pound dog. Symptoms of poisoning include restlessness, vomiting, increased heart rate, seizure, and coma. Death is possible. If your dog has ingested chocolate, you can give syrup of ipecac at a dosage of one-eighth of a teaspoon per pound to induce vomiting. Two tablespoons of hydrogen peroxide is an alternative treatment.

CHOKING

You need to open the dog's mouth to see if any object is visible. Try to hold him upside down to see if the object can be dislodged. While you are working on your dog, call your veteri-

Facing page: Applied much the same way in humans, CPR can mean the difference between life and death. This Golden Retriever is the recipient of chest compressions, which should be administered at 80 to 120 repetitions per minute.

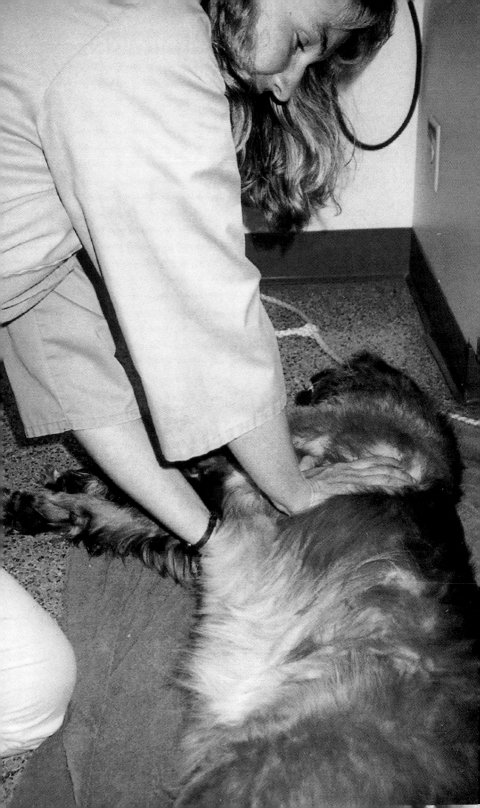

narian, as time may be critical.

DOG BITES

If your dog is bitten, wash the area and determine the severity of the situation. Some bites may need immediate attention, for instance, if it is bleeding profusely or if a lung is punctured. Other bites may be only superficial scrapes. Most dog bite cases need to be seen by the veterinarian, and some may require antibiotics. It is important that you learn if the offending dog has had a rabies vaccination. This is important for your dog but also for you, in case you are the victim. Wash the wound and call your doctor for further instructions. You should check on your tetanus vaccination history. Rarely, and I mean rarely, do dogs get tetanus. If the offending dog is a stray, try to confine him for observation. He will need to be confined for ten days. A dog that has bitten a human and is not current on his rabies vaccination cannot receive a rabies vaccination for ten days. Dog bites should be reported to the Board of Health.

DROWNING

Remove any debris from the dog's mouth and swing the dog, holding him upside down. Stimulate respiration by pulling his tongue forward. Administer CPR if necessary, and call your veterinarian.

If your dog is bitten by a strange dog or animal, a veterinarian should be sought immediately .

The risk of drowning presents itself every time your Golden enters the water, be it a lake, river, or swimming pool. If properly introduced to the water, Goldens love swimming and generally do not experience problems.

Don't give up working on the dog. Be sure to wrap him in blankets if he is cold or in shock.

ELECTROCUTION

You may want to look into puppy proofing your house by installing GFCIs (Ground Fault Circuit Interrupters) on your electrical outlets. A GFCI just saved my dog's life. He had pulled an extension cord into his crate and was "teething" on it at seven years of age. The GFCI kept him from being electrocuted. Turn off the current before touching the dog. Resuscitate him by administering CPR and pulling his tongue forward to stimulate respiration. Try mouth-to-mouth breathing if the dog is not breathing. Take him to your veterinarian as soon as possible since electrocution can cause internal problems, such as lung damage, which need medical treatment.

EYES

Red eyes indicate inflammation, and any redness to the upper white part of the eye (sclera) may constitute an emergency. Squinting, cloudiness to the cornea, or loss of vision could indicate severe problems, such as glaucoma, anterior uveitis and episcleritis. Glaucoma is an emergency if you want to save the dog's eye. A prolapsed third eyelid is abnormal and is a symptom of an underlying problem. If something should get in your dog's eye, flush it out with cold water or a saline eye wash. Epiphora and allergic conjunctivitis are annoying and frequently persistent problems. Epiphora (excessive tearing) leaves the area below the eye wet and sometimes stained. The wetness may lead to a bacterial infection. There are numerous causes (allergies, infections, foreign matter, abnormally located eyelashes and adjacent facial hair that rubs against the eyeball, defects or diseases of the tear drainage system, birth defects of the eyelids, etc.), and the treatment is based on the cause. Keeping the hair around the eye cut short around the eye and sponging the eye daily will give relief. Many cases are responsive to medical treatment. Allergic conjunctivitis may be a seasonal problem if the dog has inhalant allergies (e.g., ragweed), or it may be a year 'round problem. The conjunctiva becomes red and swollen and is prone to a bacterial infection associated with mucus accumulation or pus in the eye. Again keeping the hair around the eyes short will give relief. Mild corticosteroid drops or ointment will also give relief.

The underlying problem should be investigated.

FISH HOOKS

An imbedded fish hook will probably need to be removed by the veterinarian. More than likely, sedation will be required along with antibiotics. Don't try to remove it yourself. The shank of the hook will need to be cut off in order to push the other end through.

FOREIGN OBJECTS

I can't tell you how many chicken bones my first dog ingested. Fortunately she had a "cast iron stomach" and never suffered the consequences. However, she was always going to the veterinarian for treatment. Not all dogs are so lucky. It is unbelievable what some dogs will take a liking to. I have assisted in surgeries in which all kinds of foreign objects were removed from the stomach and/or intestinal tract. Those objects included socks, pantyhose, stockings, clothing, diapers, sanitary products, plastic, toys, and last but not least, rawhides. Surgery is costly and not always successful, especially if it is performed too late. If you see or suspect your dog has ingested a foreign object, contact your veterinarian immediately. He may tell you to induce vomiting or he may have you bring your dog to the clinic immediately. Don't induce vomiting without the veterinarian's permission, since the object may cause more damage on the way back up than it would if you allow it to pass through.

HEATSTROKE

Heatstroke is an emergency! The classic signs are rapid, shallow breathing; rapid heartbeat; a temperature above 104 degrees; and subsequent collapse. The dog needs to be cooled as quickly as possible and treated immediately by the veterinarian. If possible, spray him down with cool water and pack ice around his head, neck, and groin. Monitor his temperature and stop the cooling process as soon as his temperature reaches 103 degrees. Nevertheless, you will need to keep monitoring his temperature to be sure it doesn't elevate again. If the temperature continues to drop to below 100 degrees, it could be life threatening. Get professional help immediately. Prevention is more successful than treatment. Those at the greatest risk are brachycephalic (short nosed) breeds, obese dogs, and those that suffer from cardiovascular disease. Dogs are not able to

The curious Golden Retriever can swallow just about anything! Be careful to keep the garbage out of his way to help avoid his ingesting chicken bones or other objects that can obstruct his system.

cool off by sweating as people can. Their only way is through panting and radiation of heat from the skin surface. When stressed and exposed to high environmental temperature, high humidity, and poor ventilation, a dog can suffer heatstroke very quickly. Many people do not realize how quickly a car can overheat. Never leave a dog unattended in a car. It is even against the law in some states. Also, a brachycephalic, obese, or infirm dog should never be left unattended outside during inclement weather and should have his activities curtailed. Any dog left outside, by law, must be assured adequate shelter (including shade) and fresh water.

POISONS

Try to locate the source of the poison (the container which lists the ingredients) and call your veterinarian immediately. Be prepared to give the age and weight of your dog, the quantity of poison consumed and the probable time of ingestion. Your veterinarian will want you to read off the ingredients. If you can't reach him, you can call a local poison center or the National Poison Control Center for Animals in Illinois, which is open 24 hours a day. Their phone number is 1-800-548-2423. There is a charge for their service, so you may need to have a credit card number available.

Symptoms of poisoning include muscle trembling and weakness, increased salivation, vomiting and loss of bowel control. There are numerous household toxins (over 500,000). A dog can be poisoned by toxins in the garbage. Other poisons include pesticides, pain relievers, prescription drugs, plants, chocolate, and cleansers. Since I

own small dogs I don't have to worry about my dogs jumping up to the kitchen counters, but when I owned a large breed she would clean the counter, eating all the prescription medications.

Your pet can be poisoned by means other than directly ingesting the toxin. Ingesting a rodent that has ingested a rodenticide is one example. It is

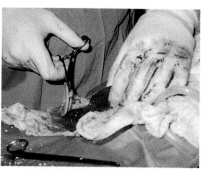

Is your home puppy-proof? Golden puppies are full of surprises. This doctor pulls a baby bottle nipple out of a puppy's intestines. Be careful about what your dog is playing with—surprises can be dangerous and costly.

possible for a dog to have a reaction to the pesticides used by exterminators. If this is suspected you should contact the exterminator about the potential dangers of the pesticides used and their side effects.

Don't give human drugs to your dog unless your veterinarian has given his approval. Some human medications can be deadly to dogs.

POISONOUS PLANTS

Amaryllis (bulb)	Jasmine (berries)
Andromeda	Jerusalem Cherry
Elephant Ear	Jimson Weed
English Ivy	Laburnum
Apple Seeds (cyanide)	Larkspur
Elderberry	Laurel
Arrowgrass	Locoweed
Avocado	Marigold
Azalea	Marijuana
Bittersweet	Mistletoe (berries)
Boxwood	Monkshood
Buttercup	Mushrooms
Caladium	Narcissus (bulb)
Castor Bean	Nightshade
Cherry Pits	Oleander
Chokecherry	Peach
Climbing Lily	Philodendron
Crown of Thorns	Poison Ivy
Daffodil (bulb)	Privet
Daphne	Rhododendron
Delphinium	Rhubarb
Dieffenbachia	Snow on the
Dumb Cane	Mountain
Foxglove	Stinging Nettle
Hemlock	Toadstool
Holly	Tobacco
Hyacinth (bulb)	Tulip (bulb)
Hydrangea	Walnut
Iris (bulb)	Wisteria
Japanese Yew	Yew

This list was published in the American Kennel Club *Gazette*, February, 1995. These are the common poisonous plants, but this list may not be complete. If your dog ingests a poisonous plant, try to identify it and call your veterinarian. Some plants cause more harm than others.

PORCUPINE QUILLS

Removal of quills is best left up to your veterinarian since it can be quite painful. Your unhappy dog would probably appreciate being sedated for the removal of the quills.

SEIZURE (CONVULSION)

Many breeds, including mixed breeds, are predisposed to seizures, although a seizure may be secondary to an underlying medical condition. Usually a seizure is not considered an emergency unless it lasts longer than ten minutes. Nevertheless, you should notify your veterinarian. Dogs do not swallow their tongues. Do not handle the dog's mouth since your dog probably cannot control his actions and may inadvertently bite you. The seizure can be mild; for instance, a dog can have a seizure standing up. More frequently the dog will lose consciousness and may urinate and/or defecate. The best thing you can do for your dog is to put him in a safe place or to block off the stairs or areas where he can fall.

SEVERE TRAUMA

See that the dog's head and neck are extended so if the dog is unconscious or in shock, he is able to breathe. If there is any vomitus, you should try to get the head extended down with the body elevated to prevent vomitus from being aspirated. Alert your veterinarian that you are on your way.

SHOCK

Shock is a life-threatening condition and requires immediate veterinary care. It can occur after an injury or even after severe fright. Other causes of shock are hemorrhage, fluid loss, sepsis, toxins, adrenal insufficiency, cardiac failure, and anaphylaxis. The symptoms are a rapid weak pulse, shallow breathing, dilated pupils, subnormal temperature, and muscle weakness. The capillary refill time (CRT) is slow, taking longer than two seconds for normal gum color to return. Keep the dog warm while transporting him to the veterinary clinic. Time is critical for survival.

SKUNKS

Skunk spraying is not necessarily an emergency, although it would be in my house. If the dog's eyes are sprayed, you need to rinse them well with water. One remedy for deskunking the dog is to wash him in tomato juice and follow with a soap and water bath. The newest remedy is bathing the dog in a mixture of one quart of three-percent hydrogen peroxide, quarter-cup baking soda, and one teaspoon liquid soap. Rinse well. There are also commercial products available.

SNAKE BITES

It is always a good idea to know what poisonous snakes reside in your area. Rattlesnakes, water moccasins, copperheads, and coral snakes are residents of some areas of the United States. Pack ice around the area that is bitten and call your veterinarian immediately to alert him that you are on your way. Try to identify the snake or at least be able to describe it (for the use of antivenin). It is possible that he may send you to another clinic that has the proper antivenin.

TOAD POISONING

Bufo toads are quite deadly. You should find out if these nasty little critters are native to your area.

VACCINATION REACTION

Once in a while, a dog may suffer an anaphylactic reaction to a vaccine. Symptoms include swelling around the muzzle, extending to the eyes. Your veterinarian may ask you to return to his office to determine the severity of the reaction. It is possible that your dog may need to stay at the hospital for a few hours during future vaccinations.

RECOMMENDED READING

DR. ACKERMAN'S DOG BOOKS FROM T.F.H.

OWNER'S GUIDE TO DOG HEALTH

TS-214, 432 pages
Over 300 color photographs

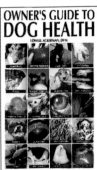

Winner of the 1995 Dog Writers Association of America's Best Health Book, this comprehensive title gives accurate, up-to-date information on all the major disorders and conditions found in dogs. Completely illustrated to help owners visualize signs of illness, different states of infection, procedures and treatment, it covers nutrition, skin disorders, disorders of the major body systems (reproductive, digestive, respiratory), eye problems, vaccines and vaccinations, dental health and more.

SKIN & COAT CARE FOR YOUR DOG

TS-249, 224 pages
Over 200 color photographs

Dr. Ackerman, a specialist in the field of dermatology and a Diplomate of the American College of Veterinary Dermatology, joins 14 of the world's most respected dermatologists and other experts to produce an extremely helpful manual on the dog's skin. Coat and skin problems are extremely common in the dog, and owners need to better understand the conditions that affect their dogs' coats. The book details everything from the basics of parasites and mange to grooming techniques, medications, hair loss and more.

DOG BEHAVIOR AND TRAINING
Veterinary Advice for Owners

TS-252, 292 pages
Over 200 color photographs

Joined by co-editors Gary Landsberg, DVM and Wayne Hunthausen, DVM, Dr. Ackerman and about 20 experts in behavioral studies and training set forth a practical guide to the common problems owners experience with their dogs. Since behavioral disorders are the number-one reason for owners to abandon a dog, it is essential for owners to understand how the dog thinks and how to correct him if he misbehaves. The book covers socialization, selection, rewards and punishment, puppy-problem prevention, excitable and disobedient behaviors, sexual behaviors, aggression, children, stress and more.

RECOMMENDED READING

GOLDEN RETRIEVER BOOKS FROM T.F.H.

THE GOLDEN RETRIEVER
by Jeffrey Pepper
PS-786, 256 pages
Color & b/w photographs

Written by well-known Golden breeder Jeffrey Pepper, *The Golden Retriever* remains a popular volume in every fancier's library. The book discusses many aspects of Golden Retriever ownership including selection, grooming, breeding, training and showing. There are many special chapters written by other breed experts, adding to the book's authority and authenticity.

THE BOOK OF THE GOLDEN RETRIEVER
by Anna Katherine Nicholas
H-1058, 480 pages
Color & b/w photographs

Nicholas, one of America's most famous dog show judges with a long-time association with the Golden Retriever, presents a thorough discussion of many foundation breeders and dogs as well as special sections on judging,

breeding, and grooming. The book remains valuable for its impressive collection of historical photographs and the information about the dogs in them.

THE WORLD OF THE GOLDEN RETRIEVER
by Nona Kilgore Bauer
TS-197, 480 pages
Over 700 color photographs

The most beautiful book ever published on the Golden Retriever is the winner of the 1994 Best Breed Book from Dog Writers Association of America authored by well-known Golden Retriever breeder, trainer and author Nona Kilgore Bauer. *The World of the Golden Retriever* brings to life this wonderful purebred, born to please and easy to love. The author's fondness for the breed is evident on every page as she discusses breed history, standard, national specialty, show ring, obedience and field trial, agility, tracking and many special areas of community work (search and rescue, therapy, guide dogs, etc.). The book also discusses the Golden in many countries around the world.